From Valley to Mountain

TWO PLAYS FROM POLITICS AND DIVINITY

DHANANJAYA KUMAR

ISBN 979-8-89519-809-4

In the Valley:

(Children's Play Inspired by Rabindranath Thakur's)

Daan Ki Mahima (Greatness in Giving)

Prasiddhi Ka Kautuk (Fame- Struck)

On the Hill:

(How Political Turmoil Gets Resolved by Divine Intervention)

(A Three – Act Play)

(An Inter – Play of Mystery, Humor, and Spirituality)

Dhananjaya Kumar

Content

In the Valley

(Page number 07 to 46)

ACT-1

Before the play begins, a bunch of kids enter the auditorium, Dancing to disco music. Then go on stage, begin to settle down in the classroom, making some comic gestures, music fades out.

SCENE-1: Social Studies classroom, about 10-15 students, settling in the class,' teacher arrives.

TEACHER: Good afternoon, everybody… Today we are gonna talk about the "lifestyle of the rich and famous" – how much money they have, how they have earned it, how they live, and what we can learn from them. Now, give some names you know of rich and famous people in America…

STUDENT – 1: The singer. His Latest album got sold 10 million copies, and he made 25 million.

STUDENT – 2: The computer guy. He made a robot to scratch your back, and it's selling fast, he already made 75 million.

STUDENT – 3: The football player. He makes 10 million every year for kicking ball

STUDENT – 4: The CEO of Poor man's insurance company. Last year his pay package was $50 million dollars, and his company made a profit of $200 million.

TEACHER: You are right… these are very rich and famous people. You see them on TV and newspapers all the time. They all have tons of money, own cool cars, private jets, soccer teams and…

STUDENT – 1: They must be eating at expensive restaurants and wearing Gucci watches.

STUDENT – 2: and Gold chains for their dogs.

TEACHER: Don't forget, what's really important is that some of them also donate lots of money to schools, hospitals and to poor people.

TEACHER: You see… they sell or do something that people are ready to pay for… And lots of people invest their money in the ideas those smart folks come up with.

STUDENT – 4: You mean people have good ideas, and other people make them rich? Don't we all have good ideas?

TEACHER: Well, some rich people don't even have great ideas; they are just born rich. But you have a good point. Anyway, tell me, some of your good ideas…

STUDENT – 5: I think people should stop fighting.

TEACHER: Now, that's a great idea; but how?

STUDENT – 5: Very simple… same way the people choose to fight; they can choose not to fight.

TEACHER: Sounds good!

STUDENT – 6: But what will happen to all those people who work in the factories that produce weapons, and those who join the army? There will be lots of jobless people if there are no wars. What do you say to that?

TEACHER: Well, they can start growing more food for the hungry, more houses for the homeless…

STUDENT – 6: … hospitals for the sick people

TEACHER: You got it!

STUDENT – 7: I have a question…

TEACHER: What's that?

STUDENT – 7: Are those people rich because they are famous, or they are famous because they are rich?

TEACHER: Any answers?

STUDENT – 7: Rich folks become famous

TEACHER: I would say both... Rich folks become famous, and famous people get rich.

STUDENT – 8: Last week we read about Mr. Mahatma Gandhi, he was very famous, was he rich too?

STUDENT – 9: And how about Albert Einstein- he had great ideas- was he a billionaire?

TEACHER: Well, well I guess some people become famous but never get rich. But most people are neither rich nor famous, like most of us... maybe one day some of you will…

STUDENT – 10: I don't care if I become rich or famous, what I really want is to be smart, nobody can stop me from becoming smart.

TEACHER: You mean to say bright?

STUDENT – 10: Now, what's the difference?

TEACHER: Well bright is what you choose to do, and smart is how you do it.

STUDENT – 10: That is smart sir.

TEACHER: Any way, what do you want to do?

STUDENT – 10: I wanna do something for my school.

TEACHER: That's nice! Schools make children smart… and bright.

STUDENT – 10: How about a music and dance festival?

TEACHER: That sounds great! But it's gonna cost some money.

STUDENT – 10: You mean no money, no festival?

TEACHER: Have you heard? Where there is a will, there is a way.

STUDENT – 11: Is that right? I am sure that's right. But it is going to be tough

TEACHER: Remember we were talking about the rich and the famous - many of them give away lots of money for good cause.

STUDENT – 11: But we don't know those people, never met them.

TEACHER: Don't give up so easily. You can start by asking your parents, and neighbors. Would be great to collect $5000.

STUDENT – 10: But how are we gonna convince them to donate?

TEACHER: That's simple promote peace. You see tell them their donation will reduce stress and music and dance is very relaxing, and musicians and dancers are very peaceful people...

STUDENT – 10: You are smart sir. We'll go for it.

(Bell rings for the end of class. Everyone begins to get up and leave)

SCENE – 2: (Lights dim… Fusion music in the background

SOUNDTRACK; While the scene changes. Same group of students milling around outside the classroom. Each one takes out some cash; one begins to count)

STUDENT – 1: Let's see, what have we got?

STUDENT – 2: We have only $210; this won't get us too far!

STUDENT – 3: Boy! It was tough getting donations…

STUDENT – 4: My dad said "you guys go to school to study – what's music and dance got to do with studies?"

STUDENT – 5: My Mom rolled her eyes and said "$5000 to sing and dance? Why not play the boom-box and start dancing?"

STUDENT – 6: I am proud of my parents- they gave me a $100 bill, cash…

STUDENT – 7: That's nice but if 50 adults had given $100 each, we would have had $5000.

STUDENT – 8: You know, I told Mr. Arnold, our neighbor, that this festival will reduce stress among students, you know what he said "what about the stress it is already giving me?"

STUDENT – 1: I knew this thing about stress is not going to work. Lot of people think that anybody who is stressed must be important.

STUDENT – 2: That's why lots of important people are sick.

STUDENT – 8: And I tried to make the point about peace with Mr. George. I said To him that our music and dance festival will promote peace. You know, his comment was… "The only way to bring peace is to kill all the violent people"

STUDENT – 4: What a way to go… more violence to produce more peace.

STUDENT – 5: Wouldn't it be great to promote peace to reduce violence?

STUDENT – 6: Isn't it great that musicians don't fight or argue that "my tune is better that your tune".

STUDENT – 2: Let's not bring religion into this.

STUDENT – 3: Look the bottom line is… this stress and peace thing did not work for collecting donations.

STUDENT – 9: I got to tell you about Mr. Chattervedayi He is one mean penny-pincher.

STUDENT – 10: Who, Chattervedayi

STUDENT – 9: You know Ravi – the freshman? That's his dad, a rich attorney. He owns 2 Mercedes and says "the market is bad, houses are not selling; no settlements, no money". That sucks Maybe we should forget about the whole thing.

STUDENT – 7: Wait, I have an idea… Let's ask these people (point to audience) if they can give $4790.

STUDENT – 8: Where does that magic number come from?

STUDENT – 7: Oh, I don't know… but that my birthday – April 7, 1990. Just kidding… Its $5000 minus $210 we already have equal to $4790.

STUDENT – 10: Ok, cut that out… I have an idea. Mr. Johnson told us that rich people donate money to feel that they are at the top of the world.

STUDENT – 9: On the top of the world.

STUDENT – 10: On or at, whatever it is. Let's push Mr. Chattervedayi to the top of the world; make him a little famous. It will be fun to see what he does. In the newsletter, you know…

(They begin to whisper... Their voices drown in the background soundtrack of fusion dance music scene change, rearrange stage props)

SCENE – 3: (After a couple of weeks. At Somesh and Seema Chaturvedi's living room. Friday evening. Somesh is pacing impatiently, looking tense. Teacher, Mr. Johnson knocks at the door, then enters the room, with a newsletter in his hand.)

SOMESH: Hello Mr... welcome, please tell me what brings you here to see me?

TEACHER: Mr. Chattervedayi, Good Afternoon! I thought, on my way back from school, I should stop by to say hello, and to thank you so much for your kindness.

SOMESH: Welcome, Welcome! What have I done?

TEACHER: Sir, first of all, I want to say that your son is doing fine at school. He has vision and leadership qualities like you.

SOMESH: OK, OK

TEACHER: Well... I want to invite you

SOMESH: I hope it's not one of your fundraising dinners.

TEACHER: No sir, we got enough funds, thanks to you.

SOMESH: Any trouble, you look tense. You know, tense people are always ready to sue somebody.

TEACHER: No, no, nothing like that. I was just hoping you will accept.

SOMESH: Accept what?

TEACHER: To be the Chief Guest at our music and dance festival.

SOMESH: Well, I don't really know enough about dance and music, where and when?

TEACHER: Actually, our students will perform at the school, at 6 pm on June 14th it's a Saturday.

SOMESH: And how much is the ticket? you know things are tight these days.

TEACHER: You don't have to worry about ticket; you have already done so much.

SOMESH: (trying to remember) you are right; I did donate $50 a couple of years ago - you know, when the market was good; everybody was on a high.

TEACHER: Well, I don't know about that; but I really appreciate the news last week.

SOMESH: Last week? I was out of town.

TEACHER: Thanks anyway (puts down the newsletter and the invitation card on the table)

SOMESH: Now tell me what would I have to do as Chief Guest? Are you going to ask for donation afterwards?

TEACHER: No sir, not again after what you have already done; but please join us for dinner afterwards.

SOMESH: Alright then, I will come. Tell me, would I have to make a speech?

TEACHER: Maybe you could say something about Indian music and dance; and a word about what inspires you to be so kind and generous.

SOMESH: OK, Mr. Johnson, have a nice weekend, see you then on the 14th.

(Teacher departs. Somesh picks up the newsletter, begins to read; phone rings.)

SOMESH: (on the phone) hello… Speaking… Oh, really?… hm… I see… yes, yes… no problem, bankruptcies are quite common these days, quite a safe way to live a good life… sure, Wednesday 10 am will be fine hm... see you then, bye.

(Mrs. Seema Chaturvedi enters the room)

SEEMA: Sam! Are you done with your meeting? New client?

SOMESH: No. Seema, that was Mr. Johnson, Ravi's teacher at Freedom High. You know, he invited me as Chief Guest at a music and dance program.

SEEMA: At the school? (Somesh nods) Chai?

SOMESH: But I can't figure out why he kept praising my kindness and generosity. That's a mystery to me.

SEEMA: (jokingly) Sam, Maybe you did something in your previous life.

SOMESH: And in this life, just taking care of you!

SEEMA: (wanders to pick up the newsletter, begins to browse)

SOMESH: OK, I will have a cup of tea with ginger and honey.

SEEMA: (appears shocked looking at the next page of newsletter) No wonder, the teacher was here, and you are the chief guest.

SOMESH: Have you solved the puzzle, tell me.

SEEMA: (looking at the paper) When did this happen? And without my knowledge?!

SOMESH: What did I do?

SEEMA: Don't look so innocent!

SOMESH: Sam, what are you talking about?

SEEMA: Look at this newsletter... "Chattervedayi pledges $5000

SOMESH: (reading the paper in amazement) Who published this? I will sue them. I am an attorney you know?!

SEEMA: Are you sure?

SOMESH: (begins to read in amazement) what's going on here? I never said anything to anybody about donating so much money, and that too for a useless activity?!

SEEMA: I know you could never do such a thing, Sam, Now I think they got you x this time, and you don't even know about it. It's the student newsletter, you know... the word is out.

SOMESH: What a prank they pulled on me! I was wondering why Mr. Johnson was so polite.

SEEMA: Wrong timing, Sam! You know we need to save up for Sonya's marriage, Ravi's college, for our retirement, to build a new home in India…

SOMESH: I can't believe this, high school kids making a fool of me!

SEEMA: So, what are you going to do about it?

SOMESH: Simple, I will call the principal with the facts - I never did nor will ever make such donations, you know, $5000 is my one whole week's income.

SEEMA: But you already accepted to be the Chief Guest... What will people think about you, your reputation, isn't that worth something?

SOMESH: I guess you are right. Tell me what do I do now? Am I stuck with this mess?

SEEMA: You don't really have a choice; Sam! Just have to go through with this. Just have to give them $ 5000, as you "promised"... And why not enjoy this fame while it lasts... feels on top of the world, as long as you can stay there.

SOMESH: You are right... I was feeling at the top of the world as long as Mr. Johnson was here.

SEEMA: I think it is "on the top of the world".

SOMESH: Whatever it is but now I feel I have fallen into this valley.

SEEMA: Don't forget- the mountain exists because of the valley.

(Seema gives a dirty look, and begins to walk out)

SCENE-4: Light dims, Somesh left alone in the room, restless, irritated, pacing around; sits in the chair, closes his eyes. (Start fog machine. Look- alike shadow, alter-ego appears through the fog, taps Somesh's shoulder)

SHADOW: (walks to SOMESH, taps his shoulder) Resting?

SOMESH: Sorry, I was dozing off… But who are you? hope you are not asking for something!!

SHADOW: I am you, your Inner Self… I already have everything, nothing to ask for.

SOMESH: Inner Self? Then, what are you doing "out" there?

SHADOW: Because, you couldn't see me "in" there.

(Light dims further; soundtrack of school music/dance program… end piece of music program fade in, fade out… audience clapping…

SHADOW: Did you enjoy the program?

SOMESH: Which program?

SHADOW: The program last week, where you were the chief guest.

SOMESH: Yes! I surely did. But how do you know know? Were you there?

SHADOW: I am everywhere all the time!

SOMESH: Now, tell me really who are you?

SHADOW: A hundred years ago my name was Narendra

SOMESH: Which Narendra? there are so many Narendras

SHADOW: Well, some people used to call me Swami Vivekananda

SOMESH: Oh! Swamiji, nice to meet you (moving in one opposite direction)

SHADOW: Why are you going away from me?

SOMESH: Oh! So sorry (turning back)

SHADOW: Now you know why I am out here! Anyway, the program was great, wasn't it? You are still intoxicated by it.

SOMESH: Yes, Swami it keeps haunting me (as if listening to soundtrack, goes back to sit in the chair)

SHADOW: You know more than a hundred years ago in America, a rich young man came to see me, a little younger than you.

SOMESH: (getting up) who was that?

SHADOW: John D. Rockefeller - very rich, very proud I told him - keep some, share some... do something for others, give back to the people, they will always remember you.

SOMESH: And, what did he do?

SHADOW: He got upset and left... but came back a week later to see me… with a list of projects he was going to finance.

SOMESH: Did he really?!

SHADOW: Yes,… that was the Rockefeller foundation, still supporting so many projects around the world today. Rockefeller is dead, his name lives on. Now get ready - it's time for your speech.

Mr. Johnson's voice (on soundtrack): Boys and girls, ladies and gentlemen! Wasn't that a great performance! Well, this program wouldn't have been possible without a generous donation from our chief guest Mr. Somesh Chattervedayi; I want to request him to please come to the mike; we want to honor him with a garland, and hear his message to our students... (more clapping).

SOMESH: (begins to get up)

SHADOW: Now you must be remembering the speech you made...

SOMESH: (In a daze) Yes, I remember

SHADOW: What did you say, let's hear it!

(shadow frozen in one spotlight, looking at Somesh)

SOMESH SPEECH: (moves towards audience, begins his chief guest speech)

Dear students and friends! I must say I can't believe this is happening, and I am standing here as chief guest... (Changing his tone). In fact, this was a great performance; and I am extremely happy to be here, supporting this great cause. In today's competitive and stressful world around us, our schools need to make special efforts to teach performing arts and cross cultural subjects to help our children develop a wholesome personality, an understanding for other peoples and cultures. Academic subjects are important, competition and excellence are also important; but that's not all. Our children also need creativity, imagination, compassion, and universal brotherhood. That is why, I couldn't refuse when some of the kids came home one day to ask for $100 donation. I told them, I will sponsor the whole program... and here's a check for $5000...

(more clapping... this speech could be longer, more punch)

SOMESH: (End of speech, goes back to chair, sits down, dozes off, soundtrack continues)

SEEMA: (on soundtrack) Wow, Sam! I like that speech! Deep stuff; I never knew you are so thoughtful; I am proud of you.

SOMESH: You know Seema, it feels good to see happy faces, like these (pointing to the audience). Makes me feel "on top of the world"

SEEMA: You mean "at the top of the world"

SOMESH: Whatever! I just want to stay there, don't want to go down. (end of soundtrack. Lights dim. Spotlight on shadow)

SHADOW: (soft laugh) Back to sleep? Far from mind! Close to heart!

(Lights out, shadow disappears, end of scene)

———◆◆———

ACT-2

SCENE-5: The CD soundtrack continues. Knock at the door; lights on; Seema opens the door

SEEMA: Hello Mr. Johnson... please come in... I really enjoyed the music and dance program the other Freedom High.

SOMESH: And I enjoyed it too much... more than I ever expected to.

TEACHER: Actually, Mr. Chattervedayi, I have come to apologize... the whole thing was so absurd. I knew the students were trying to raise funds for the program... then somewhere along the way, they got misguided and played a prank on you... one of them placed a fake announcement in the student newsletter that you have committed to sponsor the program, without your permission... that was totally unacceptable... the principal is going to take disciplinary action against them... they should be punished for such behavior...

SOMESH: Wait, let's not rush into things, we are adults.

SEEMA: I had figured out what was happening as soon as I read the newsletter.

TEACHER: And by the time I figured out, it was too late. But we cannot tolerate indiscipline - it must be punished.

SEEMA: Mr. Johnson, Somesh is a very generous person, very kind by nature. And now, he is a connoisseur of music and arts.

TEACHER: I know that now... his donation speaks a ton about his generosity.

SOMESH: That's alright Mr. Johnson! There is no need for punishment. In fact, I thoroughly enjoyed the program... and as I later discovered, I felt great about the donation, "Top of the world" you know. Please thank the kids on my behalf, I know what they did was not quite right... but I am happy they did what they did...

SEEMA: I am happy too about their mistake. I never knew this part of Somesh... was kind of hidden inside... but now I like it, and I am proud of him.

TEACHER: That's so kind of you but I am sure the principal will have to take some action.

SOMESH: I will talk to the Principal, probably go and see him... I have forgiven the students, will ask him to do the same.

TEACHER: Sir, I truly appreciate that, you are so kind and understanding; I must leave now, hope to see you again soon. By the way, here is the CD of the music program.

(Teacher departs Somesh moves toward Seema. Teacher re-enters)

TEACHER: I forgot to tell you something… We have decided to have this music and festival every year… like an annual event, you know.

SOMESH: And now that I have set a bad precedence, somebody will come back to haunt me again next year. But please, next time, make sure... No pranks!

TEACHER: Thanks in advance, Mr. Chattervedayi!

(**Teacher departs.** Somesh trying to change expression)

SOMESH: (to Seema) Did you hear what he said? Oh, never mind... So I see, you like me now...

SEEMA: I always like you… I love you. But now, I am more happy for you… you are enjoying the arts, you are more gentle and kind, more giving, more loving, more forgiving...; less stress, more peace.

SOMESH: Ok, Ok, enough… I know better what you really appreciate – I didn't know that until now...

SEEMA: You have changed Sam, and I like that. Actually, over the years, you have changed in many ways, but what I like the best is the way you are now.

SOMESH: To tell you the truth, I also like the new me, the inner me. I just need to convince myself.

SEEMA: Let me help a little. (moves closer to Somesh)

(They hold hands lovingly; Light dims)

SCENE-6: Living room. Somesh starts to play the music CD in a low volume; Seema serving tea; phone rings

SOMESH: Hello... speaking... sorry ma'am not interested... ya, ya, I know special Olympics for war veterans is a good cause, but I have to skip this time. Good bye.

SEEMA: Who was that?

SOMESH: Never mind. Herbal tea, OK! with a little bit of honey.

(phone rings again, Seema picks up)

SEEMA: Hello... yes, that's my husband, hold on

SOMESH: Yup, I am OK... what is this ADHD foundation?... I see, "attention deficit... well, I think all kids have ADHD at some point; just let them play, and learn some music and dance, they will be alright... but how did you find out about my donation to Freedom High?... Sorry sir, not this year... I have already made enough donations; and now I am also developing ADHD, can't pay attention to these things anymore... good bye.

(turning to Seema): Next time the phone rings, don't answer; at least don't pass it on to me.

SEEMA: Don't get upset! Now, you are becoming a famous… target

(Seema switches off the lamp; light dims; music fades out. After a few seconds, morning sounds on track; lights glow. Special effect - ceiling lights on/off to show passage of the day - showing Somesh and Seema in different routine situations... normal light returns. Knock on the door; Seema opens the door; a stranger standing outside)

SEEMA: Yes, hi, sorry he is busy, and he is not donating

STRANGER: Sorry to bother you ma'am; my name is Nicholas B. Damasco

SEEMA: OK, wait a moment please; I'll ask him.

(Seema goes to Somesh, who is inspecting CDs at the other side of the room)

SEEMA: Listen, there someone wanting to see you.

SOMESH: Who, what's the name?

SEEMA: Something like Nikalo Badamas ko

SOMESH: What! (laughs) Nikalo Badmas ko?!

SEEMA: Whatever! He said he will just take a minute or two. Why don't you just say hello, and sorry, and show him the road.

(Somesh approaches the door; Nicholas walks in)

NICHOLAS: Sir, I apologize for dropping in … how are you today?

SOMESH: I am fine, what can I do for you?

NICHOLAS: Well, what I heard about you is so true

SOMESH: What do you mean?

NICHOLAS: What I mean is that you are so kind and polite

SOMESH: OK! OK! Say it fast, I don't have much time.

NICHOLAS: I am one of the custodians at Freedom High School. And I can't forget the speech you made at the music and dance program.

SOMESH: Thank you… then what?

(Somesh gradually becoming irritated, as he frequently looks at his watch)

NICHOLAS: I could make out from the speech… you think well, and you are so generous.

SOMESH: OK, thanks again

NICHOLAS: And you have a heart made of gold, Sir.

SOMESH: I would be dead if that's true.

NICHOLAS: I am saying this because I was really impressed by $5000 donation for the music/dance program. But I am here for something more serious.

SOMESH: Listen, I am kinda busy...

NICHOLAS: I will just take a minute or two, sir. OK, let me come to the point. I am here on behalf of ACE

SOMESH: And what is ACE?

NICHOLAS: Association for Custodians Equality - ACE. Our goal is fight for decent pay for all custodians.

SOMESH: And what is decent pay?

NICHOLAS: Sir, right now our pay is just $25 an hour; our goal is to increase it to $50 an hour in the next 2 years.

SOMESH: Well, good luck!

NICHOLAS: We need more than good luck, sir. We need your generous donation to hire an attorney to fight our case.

SOMESH: Now, that is a serious issue. Listen, I am an attorney; and I don't think any attorney is going to take up your case. But since you kept this meeting very short, just a minute or two, here's my $10 donation; I gotta leave now.

(Somesh shows the door; Nicholas departs - looking at $10 billion with disappointment)

SOMESH: (mumbling) I wonder how many more people know about my donation! One mistake leads to another!

(Lights off. End of scene)

———••———

SCENE-7: Somesh's house, living room. Knocks at the door; Seema opens the door; a bunch of students come in, asking to see Somesh. Seema asks them to sit down, and exits.

Students move some chairs, sit on the floor-begin to sing a song.

(the song items can be lipsync to the soundtrack OR use cordless collar mikes).

(The following dialogues on soundtrack-coming from outside the room)

SOMESH: What's going on there?

SEEMA: Some kids have come from a music and dance school. They wanted to sing for you.

SOMESH: But why?

SEEMA: I don't know; but they don't want to leave without seeing you

SOMESH: Oh no, I hope they are not here to ask for money.

SEEMA: Well, let's go find out.

(Seema and Somesh enter the room; greeted by students; one of them continues to sing; another student enters hurriedly with Tabla, apologizes for being late, joins the vocalist, begins to play tabla… song continues, a few other vocalists and instrumentalists join, then music ends. Meanwhile Ravi enters, hugs parents, sits down, and makes hand movements as done by Tabla player. Students get up and greet Somesh again)

SOMESH: That was nice! Now, tell me what brings you here, other than singing… (turning to tabla student) By the way, your Tabla was good too.

TABLA Student: Sir, we are here because we heard you like music

SOMESH: And how did you hear that?

TABLA Student: A friend from Freedom High School. He was admiring your speech…

VOCAL Student: … and your donation, Sir

SOMESH: I see, I see… what did they tell you about my speech?

TABLA Student: That you spoke about "wholesome personality" and all… we also like that idea.

VOCAL Student: And they also like your donation.

SOMESH: I see, I see.

SEEMA: Looks like you have really made an impact… and a name for yourself… I told you…

(knocks at the door; a few dancers in costume enter with boombox, apologetic gesture for being late, begin to dance with soundtrack music, as other music students move to one side of the room)

SOMESH: And who are you girls?

DANCER: We are also from the same music and dance school; we heard about your speech; just had to dance for you.

SOMESH: OK, OK, go ahead… I am really beginning to enjoy all this…

(Girls play CD in boombox and begin to dance- 4-5 items. Somesh appears to enjoy a variety of dance items… claps and cheers in between... till the end. After the first dance, Sonya enters, hugs parents, sits down to watch; sometimes, she tries to make hand gestures as done by dancers)

SOMESH: That was great! I have never seen such fine performances… never knew music and dance can be so much fun! It's like being "on or at the top of the world"

STUDENTS: We are happy you like what we have learned.

SOMESH: Now, tell me about your school... what happens there?

STUDENTS: Our school is a non-profit organization (completing each others' sentences) We have classes every weekend… about 500 students… and 40 teachers… classes in Hindi and regional languages… Hindustani and Carnatic music, flute, veena, sitar, guitar, tabla, keyboard… bharatnatyam, kuchipudi, kathak, odisi, yoga, history, we have a senior club, and a youth club…

SOMESH: WOW! That's a lot of topics… kinda sounds familiar. I think I should have let Ravi and Sonya attend some of those classes too. Don't forget to invite me to your next performance… AT the school, on stage… not in this small room.

STUDENTS: (pleading, each one adds a phrase) Sir, we were hoping you would make a donation to our school, like you did to Freedom High School, please sir. You see, we are hoping to have our own building, something like the Jewish Community Center where we have classes every Sunday… right now we are renting space… not enough classes… rooms are small… we can't have classes during weeknights… sometimes, we get thrown out, sir… Please help us… And all donations are tax-exempt, Sir

SEEMA: Yes, Somesh! These kids did such a wonderful job, made you smile; you did enjoy, didn't you. Why don't you give them something… Like your one week's income!

SOMESH: Seema! what are you saying? Let me at least think about it... you know I am not used to... (turning to students) OK, boys and girls - thanks for the show... see you soon.

STUDENTS: Sir, we hope you won't forget us... we have brought a small present for you.

(They present a box containing a CD of their music program, a book "Natya Shastra" by sage Bharata, and a card which reads "To Mr. Somesh Chatturvedi, a great benefactor of music and dance". Somesh is happy, inspects the gift box; Seema is pleased; they hold hand lovingly; Students depart. Somesh begins to play the CD, as light dims end scene, Room to be rearranged)

SCENE-8: Seema and Somesh return. Somesh starts to play the CD again; music resumes in sequence, picks up a book again, then puts the book down, closes his eyes, music continues.

SOMESH: (after a couple of minutes, opens his eyes, looks at Seema) You know, I have been thinking… about life, money, we are getting older; I can retire next year if I want to…

SEEMA: So, you are resting or thinking.

SOMESH: Yes, I was thinking… why not we plan to retire… apply for social security… travel to some nice places like New Zealand, and of course India - the Himalayas…

SEEMA: Sounds good! Looks like those kids have had quite an impact on you.

SOMESH: Yes, they have… But, all these thoughts are making me restless.

SEEMA: Nothing wrong with planning the future.

SOMESH: Yes, I was saying… we don't need this big house, perhaps sell the other 2 properties… we can move into smaller house or condo… and God will take care of us.

SEEMA: Really! Are you sure? And who will take care of me?

SOMESH: Yes, God plus the money we will have left... will take care of both of us.

SEEMA: Now, I can tell what you are thinking.

SOMESH: You are right Seema... Keep some, share some.

SEEMA: Just imagine! If folks with money didn't give, didn't share... many people sitting here wouldn't be here.

SOMESH: I know, I know... most private colleges, hospitals, scholarships, all exist because many people with money...

SEEMA: have good hearts... and many things remain to be done for peace, environment, poverty, culture...

SOMESH: But I am sick and tired of being bugged by people calling and showing up for donations. I want to close that chapter and live in peace.

SEEMA: What do you mean?

SOMESH: You know I have been thinking about those kids who came to sing and dance for us the other day... they were so calm, peaceful, and intelligent. Without the school and the cultural center they were talking about, the whole field of classical music and dance may one day become extinct.

SEEMA: That is quite possible… would be such a great loss.

SOMESH: That's why, I have decided to donate $500,000 to the cultural center, where they can continue to teach more music and dance. That will be our gift to future generations. You see, I just don't want to think about being at the top of the world, I want to actually experience it, in life and in death.

SEEMA: Now, that's going too far… you are making me worried… what will happen to me and the kids? Have you thought about that?

SOMESH: Well, there is still enough left for you. And the kids… I am sure they will do well in life.

SEEMA: Looks like the speech at the school has changed you completely, Sam.

SOMESH: (looking skyward) It's not the speech Seema; it's the "dream" after the speech… and what Narendra told me…

SEEMA: (looks puzzled) Dream? What dream?

(lights fade; the end)

(meanwhile in the dark, Bhangra dancers spread out in the auditorium. Music begins, all lights on. Dancers engage the entire audience. CREDITS)

❖❖

On the Hill

(Page number 47 to 137)

SAHARA
In collaboration with The India Development & Relief Fund (IDRF), the India International School of Virginia, and the India Cultural Coordination Committee (ICCC) proudly presents
ON THE HILL
(A Three-Act Play in English)
AN INTERPLAY OF MYSTERY, HUMOR AND SPIRITUALITY: THE PLAY DELVES INTO THE LIVES AND ASPIRATIONS OF ASIAN INDIANS IN MAINSTREAM AMERICA
Story, Script, Music and Direction by
Dhananjaya Kumar
Producer
Pushpa Dashottar
Co-Director
Suma Muralidhar
Starring: Walter Andersen, Amitayush Bahri, Sonya Chawla, Vera Chawla, Jon Gann, Raj Hajela, Harkesh Manocha, Karen Molchany, Geff Murphy, Donna Newton, Noor Naghmi, Pranav Pandya, Paresh Parekh, Varun Tandon & Gopal Yadav
APRIL 12, 13 AT 8:00 PM
& APRIL 14 AT 4:00 PM
F. SCOTT FITZGERALD THEATRE
ROCKVILLE, MARYLAND
(for directions, please call 301-309-3007)
Minimum Donation: $10 per person
Contributions to SAHARA are tax-deductible • Net proceeds will be distributed to charities in India and the USA
FOR FURTHER INFORMATION, PLEASE CALL:
T. Srikantaiah 301-530-4511
Renu Suri 301-330-0418
Inder Chandra 703-569-2276
Radhika Yadav 703-256-7115
Vijay Deshpande 301-596-1910
Pushpa Dashottar 301-984-1674
Renuka Misra 301-330-5098
Alka Rastogi 703-503-6051
Rajesh Nandan Parthasarathy 000-000-0000
Suma Muralidhar 301-530-5057
Vinod Prakash 301-984-2127
Rajiv Sarin 703-644-0356
Satya Ray 301-948-8069

Parallel Themes

1. **John's Biography:** Story of John's humble beginning in a small Indian town; then moving on to Delhi, to USA, to higher education, to successful career, to high political office. Parents have returned to India. Happy family and public status. Yet he is searching for meaning to life and answers to its yearning questions.

2. **Sequential Transformation:** From village to town to big city to Western affluence. From farm life to higher education to urbanization to Westernization. From basic needs to luxurious lifestyle. From modest origin to the helm of power and prosperity. Yet the level of inner happiness and satisfaction seems elusive, and independent of material abundance.

3. **Search for Identity and Spiritual Realization:** All external stimuli are fleeting. Spirituality must be found within one self. Dependence on external forces and gratification is only transient. However, external factors sometimes prove to be a channel to light the path and pave the way for inner search.

4. **<u>Personal Isolation Deprives Appreciation of Social Issues:</u>** Often in the absence of personal experience and involvement, the costs of social disharmony remain unrecognized by most individuals. Audience curiosity regarding Misha's incomplete class presentation remains unsatisfied due to the intervention of school violence. They would wish that the disturbance didn't occur and the presentation was allowed to be completed, and are forced to think why it wasn't. This offers a glimpse into the direct, personal cost of an existing problem. Similarly, they would wish that Raju was spotted when and where he was being sought.

5. **<u>Spiritual and Divine Pursuits have an Important Role in Life:</u>** Having tasted a glimpse of divine presence, individuals would find it difficult to abandon spirituality in their lives. Without spiritual growth, life's journey becomes stationary and devoid of higher and more permanent levels of bliss and realization.

6. **<u>Mythological Story:</u>** John's conscience and curiosity produce a supernatural response. Raju appears in John's life to inspire and lead, and disappears when the time has come for John to seek his own inner self. Later, John's inability to locate Raju points to a temporary, super-human presence.

7. **<u>Inter-Cultural:</u>** Story of conflicts and adjustments among Indian and American values, especially in respect of social interactions, raising the children, and pursuit of personal happiness.

8. **<u>Social Commentary:</u>** Tackles some of the pressing social problems and points to preventive solutions. Also brings home the costs of inaction or misdirected action. Humor and satire are employed to bring home a multiplicity of ideas.

9. **<u>Tip of the Iceberg:</u>** Touches upon numerous dimensions of life and thought; and fires curiosity among the audience for a must fuller picture which is there, but which they complete on their own. The inter-play of several parallel emotions induces the audience to dig deeper into each question.

10. **<u>"Sagar manthan":</u>** The primordial churning is ever present in our lives, churning social issues as well as our own minds. Through individual consciousness, one is able to seperate the byproducts of Manthan, Poison and nectar and make choices where personal and social goals converge.

———◆◆———

Characters

There are nine main characters- six Indian and three American. In addition, there are about 8-10 teenage Americans in a high-school classroom scene. They can also fill in as the stage audience in the opening scene. The manthan action scene is to be performed by a group of dancers. Also needed are: a group for staff for the Senator's campaign office; a dummy of Rishi-1, and a real video technician-cum-photographer.

Rajesh Nandan Parthasarathy (Raju): 13-14 years old student visitor from India; good manners; innocent charm; humorous; inquisitive and suggestive; smiling face; spiritual appearance; presence of mind; some Indian accent; plays flute; calm and soothing presence; has no strong reactions; wears shorts and collar-less t-shirt; has curly hair. He exudes natural familiarity with the topics of his dialogues, although those topics are complex and philosophical. His personality should impart credibility to his character. He evolves from being child-like in ACT-2 to seriousness in ACT-3. Overall, Raju is more like an idea, rather than a human character.

<u>Senator Arjun Pandey (John)</u>: Mid 40's; Indo-American in style and mannerism; well-dressed and elegant. Recently elected as Senator; highly motivated to do good; sometimes unsure and frustrated; very intelligent and confident; strong personality; slightly subdued in front of Raju; continually exposed to conflicts and dilemma; proud to be Indian but reluctant to admit; strong seeker of inner strength and meaning. He has come a long way from a humble beginning to the height of power and prestige. Everyone in the audience should be able to identify with aspects of his personality, and events in his life. He exposes his inner feelings only to Raju. He is subconsciously attracted to Debby. He evolves from being a confident politician on video in ACT-1 and early part of interview with Debby, to someone who doesn't know all the answers, to a humble seeker in front of Raju and an imperfect householder in ACT-3. Appears in all scenes except classroom. His acceptance speech is on video in ACT-1. Overall, John's character encompasses many aspects of a noble humanity. Audiences should be able to identify with parts of his personality and character.

<u>Gauri Pandey- Senator's wife</u>: Late 30's; self-centered; good housewife; socialite; status-conscious; sophisticated; fun- loving; quite Westernized but likes to demonstrate being an Indian; a step removed from John's inner journey. First she is proud of John's success and supportive of his work, but gradually becomes resentful as she feels the family and herself being neglected. She does not give any indication of having any marital problems with John. Attaches priority to family and household matters; not interested in deeper issues. She evolves from being proud of John, to complains and self-pity, to being a martyr for John. Appears in ACT-2 Scene-1, and in ACT-3.

<u>Misha Pandey- Senator's daughter:</u> 16-17 years old; darling daughter; bright and serious; confident and assertive; thoughtful and incisive; wellrounded and well-grounded. She is normally calm, but a bit agitated by interruptions in the classroom. With Vicki, she only pretends to be annoyed from time to time. Appears in ACT-2 and ACT-3.

<u>Vikram (Vicki) Pandey- Senator's son):</u> 7-8 years old; loving and sloppy; always happy. Occasionally, gives cute answers to complex questions. He evolves from being a cute kid in ACT-2, to an aggressive demeanor in the kidnap scene in ACT-3, to becoming the torchbearer of Raju in the end. He is childlike in ACT-2, but becomes serious after Raju's departure in ACT-3. Appears in ACT-2 Scene-1, and in ACT-3.

<u>Deborah (Debby) Perkins- journalist:</u> Early 30's; very bright; knowledgeable; strong professional ethics and appearance; asks difficult questions; atypical journalist. Usually cold, but warms up to John subconsciously. She evolves from being a tough journalist to a sympathizer and admirer of John. Appears on stage and video film in ACT-1, and again in ACT-3.

Stanley Soloman: Business lobbyist. Late 40's. Polished; argumentative; imposing personality. Well dressed. Formal and elegant. Tough demeanor when talking about John, but respectful when talking directly to John. Stanley is in essence the anti- thesis of John. Appears only in ACT-3.

Chris Bennett (teacher): Mid 30's; history teacher; stone-faced but friendly; bookish but funny; very lively; relates well with students. Appears in ACT-2 Scene-2.

Munshi: Late 40's; a bit clumsy; variable moods; heavy Indian accent; dressed in Dhoti, Kurta, Nehru jacket, and glasses. Known by his nasal hehe-he. Appears only in ACT-3.

8-10 High-School Students: 16-17 years old; smart but sometimes rash; Occasional ignorance or misdemeanor seems deliberate. 4-5 boys; 4-5 girls. Mostly Caucasian, one black boy, one oriental girl. Appear only in ACT-2 Scene-2; can fill in for other small roles in ACT-1. Misha is the only Indian in class. Raju accompanies Misha to the class.

Video Technician: Late 30's; long hair; informal dress. Appears only in ACT-1; no dialogue.

Rishi: Divine sage; long hair and beard; a bit short-tempered; heavy voice. Appears only in ACT-1.

Dancer: 12-14 years; proficient dancer; divine looks; meaningful smile; tells a story through her dance movements and facial expressions. Appears only in ACT-1.

Lakhan: Mid 30's; peon-style. Appears in ACT-3.

Campaign Staff: Casually dressed; stressed; anxious. Appear only on video film in ACT-1.

Anchorman: Appears only on video in ACT-1.

Masked Characters: (Freedom, Government, Democracy, Justice) Distinct and mysterious. Each has own style and mannerism. Appear only in ACT-3.

Group of dancers: two groups dressed and move differently. Appear in Manthan action scene in ACT-1.

—●●—

ACT-1

(Soundtrack... Opening cosmic music begins... fades after one minute... 10 seconds gap... Recital of Vedic Mantras begins, then ends. Voices of struggle fade in... Manthan music superimposed... soundtrack fades out... then total silence, still dark. Curtain remains closed. Now silence is broken by voices of celebration- Indian and American- and office noise plus picture on big screen shows the following intermittent conversation. Projections on big screen shows 5 interconnected video clips: John's campaign office, anchorman's announcement of his election victory, Debby's cue for John; John's acceptance speech, followed by Debby's narration of John's background. These are synchronized with soundtrack; shot in video format. Stereo sound is used to seperate left and right channels, or left and right side of stage. Curtain still remains closed. Campaign office and 4-6 staff workers are seen on screen. Anxiety and anticipation in the atmosphere.

<u>STAFF#1:</u> (medium shot of office from entrance door; then camera opposite the door shows ONE entering office, pacing, while others are busy; some are sitting and some standing) Hello... everybody! How is it going?

(Moving shifts, Standing, moving)

STAFF#2: Well, we have done our part. (looks at his watch) Hey, the vote counts must be coming in... let's tune in and watch the election results. (turns on the office TV shown as video-in-video; gesture everyone to watch; some pictures are seen, but no sound; anchorman seen in news type broadcast)

(standing, Turns on TV, no sound still)

STAFF#1: Look! It might take a while for the TV guys to get the final count... What do you think is going to happen?

(observe T1)

STAFF#2: Well, just cross your fingers and pray.

STAFF#3: (gets up and offers to serve) Bhai aap log kuchh kha lo, samosa... chai... sab taiyar hai. Let me fix that. (others respond "No, thanks" "Don't worry, we will help ourselves")

(points to stairs)

STAFF#1: Pushpajil you know, we will starve without you. (gets up for tea, takes a sip, sits down) Just imagine... What if we won the election!

(moves to push to sits)

STAFF#4: (contemplative, gets up for tea but prepares it very slowly while speaking) People are so fed up, they might just vote for us for a change; to try a totally new man, a different kind of man... not married to any ideology... not part of any vote bank in the Senate. No party line... no baggage... no nonsense.

STAFF#5: Well, Johny Pandey is a smart man; his ideas deserve support. I think people do like him, they will like him. They will dig his mind... love his words.

STAFF#3: (involved in samosa and tea) Bahut himmat hai Arjun bhai mein... bas aa gaye maidan mein. Look at his courage, confidence, and above all... his charisma.

STAFF#1: You know, I have a feeling he will win.

STAFF#4: I think so too, let's have our champagne bottles ready.

STAFF#1: Wait a minute... champagne isn't important. We will make history if we win.

STAFF#4: Who cares about history, we are going to make the future.

STAFF#3: Sabse badi baat hai ki ab apna admi pahunch jayega safed ghar mein. Finally, we will have our own man on the Hill.

STAFF#2: I hope you are right, he will do a better job than many of them.

STAFF#5: Well, even if he does nothing that will still be better than some of them.

STAFF#4: But John wouldn't be happy doing nothing; he will make a difference, I am sure. Don't you think so?

STAFF#4: Absolutely. But you know something?... (voice drowns)

(Video picture continues, but Manthan music fades in on video soundtrack and drowns the voices, then fades out. Five seconds silence.

STAFF#2 goes to adjust TV and discretely pushes play button VCR. Video camera focused on office TV, then zooms in to enlarge the picture which now covers then large screen on stage. GNN signature sound picks up with logo on office TV screen. TV news in male voice begins on close-up of office TV screen):

Anchorman: We have an unusual election victory tonight… Mr. Airjoan Pandee has been elected to the US Senate as an independent candidate from Maryland. We now have a special report live from Pandee's campaign headquarters, with our political correspondent- Deborah Perkins… Debby!

(office TV scene is cut. Debby appears on big screen.)

Debby: (on screen, with a tiny smile; campaign office background) There is much to celebrate at Airjoan Pandee's camp tonight. He looks tired but joyous among his supporters. Here's a live coverage of his acceptance speech. (background noise. Then big screen changes)

John: (on screen) tired but happy expression; campaign office background; political speech mode) Fellow Americans! I am happy and grateful that you have chosen me to serve this great nation of ours. My victory is your victory. Tonight you have shown to the world that we are capable of putting aside our ethnic differences to pursue our larger interests and bigger goals.

(John flanked by straters & Family outside decorate office. Inside office…

Let us capitalize on our inner strengths to solve the problems facing us today; and build a society free from fear, hatred and isolation. I know we can, and will do it, together… (sound of cheers). I again want to thank our campaign staff, all those people who supported us and also those who criticized us, for making this possible. Thank you, and God bless America. (cheers up and fade; picture on big screen changes to Debby)

(From wide angle showing John & other to focus on Debby)

Debby: (on screen; reporting mode; campaign office background) You've just watched the acceptance speech by Senator-elect Airjoan Pandee. Pandee was born in 1962 to a farming family in a small town called Singapore, sorry make that Rangapore in india Pandee was a child when his parents migrated to the US in 1978. He was first exposed to public life and politics when his father became a strong supporter of Dr. Martin Luther King, Jr., and joined the civil rights movement in the 1960's. Airjoan Pandee received his MBA from Duke University in 1987. And over the next 10 years, held management positions in several large corporations. The entire Pandee family lived together until 1992 when his ageing parents decided to return to India to retire on their farm. Airjoan Pandee now lives in Bethesda, Maryland with his wife and two children. I am sure in the coming weeks, you will be hearing a lot more from and about the Senator-elect. From his campaign headquarters, this is Debby Perkins reporting. Back to you, Walter.

(Screen projection now ends, cheering noises up and fade.)

Manthan music begins. Curtain opens; after 1 minute music blends with manthan action background which is shown as live action in rear stage in front of flood lights facing large light blue backdrop. Things being churned out and snatched.

(M – 3 end Manthan edition also ends)

Manthan actions flashes whenever lightning effect happens on stage, unless otherwise specified. Left half of stage has 10-12 chairs. Rishi-1 is the only one sitting in chair. Rishi-1 is actually a dummy, with Raju hidden inside.

Would-be audience including Rishi enter roaming around the Then stage, with soundtrack of chorus humming Mantras. Each one crowd has different costume and mannerism to represent diverse population. A few people gradually take their seats; others keep walking around aimlessly. Chorus humming ends. Two people enter from right stage with a long white bedsheet, try to wrap around and scoop those still walking, and try to remove them from stage, saying):

"You are not part of this play, you must clear the stage. You don't belong here. The show has already begun. You have to leave... now"

(A few more now join the stage audience; others leave after minor struggle. Light on stage audience at left stage slowly dims. Manthan action continues without sound. One minute silence; and in his Senate office. These clips end. Right stage spot appears on John and

Debby. They are facing the audience; John is sitting to the left of Deby. Global News Network (GNN) interview about to begin. Mini studio set up with video camera and technician. Big screen monitor for the audience. There are two signature music pieces. One for Manthan or whenever serious questions arise or judgement is required by John. The other is flute piece for Raju's entry or rememberance. The flute piece is also played back by Raju with soundtrack synchronization in Act-3. The following interview should have frequent changes in tempo and intonation to avoid any impression of dullness. Also note that deeper dialogues during parts of the interview below, and Raju-John conversation in ACT-3, should be delivered slowly and emphatically to ensure being understood, at least clearly heard, by the audience. Breakfast scene and John-Munshi dialogues can be slightly accelerated)

Debby: (facing camera and appearing on big screen) Good evening, and Welcome to Global News Network. I am Deborah Perkins, your host for this Special Edition on American Politics. Today, we have in our studio Senator Airjoan Pandee- the first Asian Indian to be elected to that office. (Debby and camera turn to John) Senator! Did I pronounce your name correctly?

John: (happy face) Thank you Debby! Actually, it's very easy... ARJUN Arjun. PANDEY Pandey. Arjun Pandey, or you can simply call me John for short, like my friends do.

Debby: Thank you, Senator. And welcome again to this Special Edition of GNN.

John: (broad smile) Thanks again Debby! I am glad to join your show and share some thoughts with the American people.

Debby: (interview mode) Senator! Please tell our viewers- how does feel to be the first Asian Indian to be elected to the US Senate?

John: (political speech mode) I am indeed very happy, and thank my constituents for giving me this opportunity. I also want to point out, Debby, that being first is nothing new or unusual for our country. We are the first in the whole world in economic and military power; we are always the first to respond to natural or man-made calamities anywhere in the world; we are the first choice for immigrants from distant lands; (slight skepticism) we are the first in technology, work ethics, honesty, and charity. Our country is the first choice even for people to fall sick (humor)... Being the first Asian Indian to become Senator makes me proud to be part of such a rational and democratic tradition, and be able to serve the American people.

Debby: (questioning mode) what about the ethnic Asian Indian community, Senator? What do you hope to do for them?

John: (slightly taken aback) Well... I will... certainly serve their interests... (now with confidence) to the extent that they are part of the American mainstream.

Debby: (probing mode) Do you intend to take a special interest in promoting the welfare of Asian Indians... or in building better relations between India and the United States? Do you plan to sponsor any legislation these areas?

(Manthan music picks up. A lightning effect on left stage shows flashes of Manthan action.)

John: (looks around as if attention is diverted, then hesitatingly) Well... Yes, of course... I am sure there will be opportunities to look into those areas.

Debby: (notices John's discomfort without comment) OK, Senator, to many of our viewers, crime is the number one problem facing the American society today. Our President is so serious about it, he has even called for a major conference on crime. One of your campaign promises was to work out a program to solve this problem. Please tell our viewers what you plan to do?

John: (anticipated question; ready answer) If we want to solve our social problems, including crime, the best place to begin is to focus on the causes rather than symptoms. We can not solve our problems by throwing money at them. As you know, seeds are known to grow through the rocks. Therefore, our first step should be to take a close look at our education system, both in school and at home. We need to teach our children social responsibility and model behavior. They must learn to sacrifice a small part of their freedom, if necessary, to protect the freedom of other people; and to ensure a coherent and peaceful society. That is why, Debby, first on my agenda is to work on an education reform bill.

Debby: Are you saying, Senator, that our children are not getting a good enough education?

John: (diplomatic mode) Debby, of course, our children are getting good technical education. They learn to compete; but I think they also need to learn to complement, cooperate and accommodate. We need an education system which teaches family values, self-respect and respect for others, the value of sacrifice and tolerance, preservation rather than destruction, persistence rather than desperation. An education system which presents good role models, and prepares our children to be compatible, compassionate and cooperative members of our society.

Debby: (attack mode) But, Senator! All that is for the future generation. How do we solve the problems of crime and terrorism today? We know that weapons kill; but weapons also protect. And everybody needs protection... what should we be do?

John: Well... as we all know, mankind today has more weapons than ever before. But my question is-

Debby: Are you saying that we should reduce defense? If so, how do you intend to convince the Congress and the President that Americans will be just as safe with lessee defense?

(Manthan music, lightning... disturbs John. He begins to look around; visibly distracted from the interview.)

John: (distraction as pretext) Listen... I am hearing some noises... now getting louder. Please do something about it.

Debby: I don't really know where it's coming from. Anyway, I will have our sound engineer check it out. (video technician takes clue from Debby to check wires and connections, then gestures OK) let's get on with our interview... Senator, you have made speeches about protecting the environment, and---

John: (jokingly) of course, these days, everybody makes speeches about the environment. But, as usual, speeches don't solve anything.

<u>Debby</u>: (reasserts) You are right... and, they all don't sound coherent either. Now let me ask you another question what do you think about the American people's fascination with the ancient Indian techniques of yoga, meditation, and the mind-body medicine or psycho-neuroimmunology?

<u>John</u>: (trying to be coherent; doesn't mean what is said) I am glad that American scientists have validated the benefits of these things; otherwise we would have lost a great body of knowledge. Same way that the Indian classical music has been preserved through Western interest in it over the past hundred years.

(Manthan is grinding louder, red and blue light on left stage to distinguish gods and demons. Action is now more visible. Both John and Debby get diverted)

<u>John</u>: (disinterested in interview, pointing to the other side of stage) Now I can see something... I can hear something... There is a struggle of some sort. (begins to get up, but sits down again) What do you think that is, Debbie?

<u>Debby</u>: (salvage mode) I don't know. I am more concerned about making our program interesting to our viewers. Same way as you need to win votes. But Senator, our interview isn't over yet. I have one last question for you. Senator... You have talked about the problem of poverty in America. There is illiteracy. There are homeless people. Many elderly and disabled people are also poor. Some call them the unfit people in our society. What can and should be done about them? Can society afford their survival? If so, who should pay and how?

John: (disturbed and diverted) Insert A, Debby, do you see that? Hear that? (getting up) I am sorry, but I must find out... before I can answer any more questions. (leaves GNN studio)

Debby: (into the camera; trying to appear calm) We'll be back, don't go away. (GNN music resumes)

(GNN music is drowned in Manthan music, which continues softly Spot off the mini studio. Debby and technician sit still. Spot moves with John. John moves across stage a few times. In effect, he is seen switching spot follows john. across the two sides- gods and demons- differentiated by golden and blue lights. Left stage light slightly up, John pauses near Rishi2 and watches in amazement. The stage audience does not notice John.)

John: (hesitatingly) Excuse me! Could you please tell me what is going on here? (Getting no response, repeats his question) I am sorry to disturb you... forgive me for being so curious... please tell me what is all that? I have never seen anything like that before.

Rishi: (irritated, slowly turns to John) Can't you see?... the gods and the demons are churning the ocean... (turning back to Manthan) I want to see what is coming out and who is getting what... and which side is winning. (brushes John aside, and resumes his gaze)

John: (confused) But all I can see is the struggle... who are the gods... and who are the demons? Why are they here? And where are they?

Rishi: That you can see only from where I sit. This is an age-old struggle... not over yet... still going on. Been sitting here... watching... patiently... since the dawn of time.

John: (lighter moment) Oh, I see. But you don't look that old. (no response; apologetic) I am sorry... (trying to refocus on Manthan action) I can hear clearly... but can hardly (Manthan music stops, but action continues) Now I don't even hear anything. Why don't you tell me, I need help... please.

Rishi: (heavy tone with smile) The sight and the sound... all are there. It's just that... your eyes and ears are weak.

John: (puzzled) You mean to say... my senses are not good enough? What should I... what can I do about that?

(No response from Rishi-2. Stage audience sitting still. Quiet everywhere. John- embarassed by his movements- goes to everyone reluctantly, asks similar questions, but gets no response. Finally, goes slowly to Rishi-1)

<u>John:</u> (pathetic) oh, sage, your holiness! I don't see; tell me what I don't hear. is happening in the ocean? Is there one? imagining it? (no response from Rishi-1. Please show me what Where is God? What Or I am just Light dims) Why me? Please tell this darkness? Why so much is hidden from me... I need to know... I must find out. (still no response) Your silence is killing me, oh sage. How long will I have to stay in the dark? Tell me please... I need help, or I will go blind.

(John gets frustrated. Begins shaking Rishi-1's shoulders. Some in the stage audience look irritated, and gesture John to stop. John continues. Rishi-1 collapses and falls flat on stage, with a thumping sound. John is stunned, appears incriminated. Raju emerges from dummy of Rishi-1, looks at John with a smile, then exits stage. John is puzzled, and raises hands up in the air... moves around the stage searching... seen as pausing on the side of gods...

Manthan audience staring at and pointing to, John in accusation. Silence Debby and the technician are now also seen as watching in amazement. They get up, begin to move toward John, but reluctant to go closer. They gesture disgust and walk out, Walk out, while John gestures them to stop.

Rhythmic music for dance begins. A young girl- 10-12 years old- enters dancing, carrying a Kalash (pitcher). John is puzzled, curious, apprehensive. After a few rounds of dance movement (2-3 minutes), the girl comes close to John and attempts to pour water in his hands. John moves back, spills the water. Dance music stops abruptly... Girl exits in disappointment.

John moves slowly toward girl, makes gesture to stop her. John gives up and is shook up as if his last hope is dwindling. Spot appears on him as stage light dims. He clinches his fists, closes his eyes, facing skyward.

Chorns humming begins.

Manthan audience gets up & begins to move toward John, enter spot then freezes. Curtain close. End of Act-1. Duration 25-30 minutes.

ACT-2: SCENE-1

(A few months have passed. Morning time, Senator's living room, birds chirping, golden light on stage, and morning Raga effects. Curtain opens. Preparations for breakfast. Misha is setting up table; Vicki is reading his book)

Gauri: (walks in, looks around, pacing… addresses Misha) Now that you can prepare breakfast, I want you to start learning to cook dinner… (pauses pensively) I hadn't imagined that our lives would change so much, so soon after your father became senator.

Misha: How come, Mom?

Gauri: Don't you see how busy he is… he doesn't even have time to read his favorite books… Or enjoy his favorite music… Or talk to us like he used to. (pauses to fix something) Even when he is at home, his mind is somewhere else. You see, he is always trying to do something. And he gets worried when things don't happen right or fast enough. He also gets disappointed with himself... and when other people don't see his vision or share his ideas.

Vicki: (trying to memorize to himself a verse by Rudyard Kipling)

"I keep six honest serving men, they taught me all I knew Their names are what and why and when and how and where and who"

Misha: (stops what she is doing) But he does get a lot of attention and importance. Isn't that right, mom?

Gauri: (stays busy, keep mumbling yes, He likes all that, but still feels lonely sometimes. If I knew all this, I would never have let him go into politics. We were happy as we were, but he was restless... Wanted to change things, and do something meaningful. Let's hope he finds the meaning he is looking for. I hope there is a way to make him happy... prove his worth.)

Vicki: (munching chocolate chip cookies, dropping, picking) Mom, I think dad should quit his job and stay home with us.

Misha: Are you crazy? First, why don't you quit eating junk, before he quits his job.

(Vicki looks apologetic, puts cookies away, and returns to his book. Misha exits to bring more stuff.)

<u>Vicki:</u> (softly) I keep six honest serving men...

<u>Gauri:</u> (lovingly) Look Vickil If daddy quits his job, how can we afford to live in this big house, have two nice cars, buy you expensive designer clothes, and eat out every Friday night? Maybe, when you grow up, you can take care of us.

<u>Vicki:</u> (assertively) I will... mom. When I grow up, I will make lots of money, and buy everything we need. Then daddy wouldn't have to work; he can then stay home and play with me, right?

<u>Gauri:</u> Right... but first you need to study hard, grow up to be a smart man, like your dad... (retracts) well, may be not quite that smart; (resumes) and then you can take care of us. Until then, we have to take care of you.

<u>Vicki:</u> That's why I am learning this poem my English teacher asked me to memorize. (repeats the verse by Kipling)

<u>Gauri:</u> (lighthearted) Vicki, that's good, you've got it. (hugs and kisses Vicki) Now go take a shower and get ready for school. And listen! tell daddy and Raju to get ready for breakfast.

(Vicki exits playfully, almost bumps into Misha who is entering with tea pot and milk bottle. Comic music piece to match the events, followed by sound of shower.)

Misha: (annoyed) Vicki, watch out... be heard saying "sorry" from backstage) tone) Mom, Raju is such a cute boy. careful. (Vicki is (now changes to soft (flute music fades in softly) Vicki loves to play with him. You know mom, Raju told us some fascinating stories. I wonder where he learned all that. And I love the way he plays the flute. Have you heard him, mom?

Gauri: sigh of relief) You are right... Remember? All of a sudden, one day last month, we get a call from some school principal in India that one of his students wants to visit USA, and if our family could host him for the summer. I don't know how he got our contact, but I said... OK. (looks puzzled, then changes expression, and moves to set up plates and cutlery) Now I am glad I did. Your daddy is so happy Raju is with us. Sometimes, after we go to sleep, your daddy and Raju stay awake, and keep talking about something or the other. I can't imagine what all he talks about with that boy for so long... more than he talks to us...

Misha: (stops what she is doing, and reinforces Mom's point) Yeah... One day, I overheard them talking about the Bible and the Gita. Another time, they were talking about Deborah Perkins... and all the questions she was asking dad on the TV interview.

Gauri: (concerned) I wonder what your dad would have done, if Raju hadn't come here this summer. In just a few weeks, he has become like part of our family. Maybe we should adopt Raju and keep him with us. Do you think he will stay?

(Flute music fades out, after Raju enters calmly, smiling)

Misha: (lively) Good morning Raju... breakfast is ready.

Raju: Good morning didi, good morning auntie. Where is Vicki?

Gauri: He is getting ready for school.

Raju: (emphasis) And where's uncle? Let's wait for him, before we start eating. I will read the news (sits down on couch; reading newspaper; pause; then suddenly) Auntie, look! this newspaper has only bad news.

Misha: (sarcastically) Yeah, the whole paper looks like the Metro Section.

Raju: Don't ve get another newspaper... the good-news newspaper?

Gauri: (paranoid) They are all the same, Raju. It seems bad news is the only news there is. Plus there are endless ads for everything they think we must have. Look at all the good-looking health-food ads... after some time, somebody will write a book about all the diseases these health-foods are responsible for.

Misha: (serious) Maybe, as the theory goes, if they cut down on printing the bad news, there will be less bad news to print. Maybe, dad should talk to Debby about it.

Gauri: (changing subject) Alright... so... uncle and you have become great buddies... eh? I hear you tell him lots of stories, and he likes to hear them.

Raju: Auntie! You know something? that's the only reason I...

John: (enters holding Vicki) Good morning everybody. (everyone responds) Here's our official alarm clock (puts Vicki down) And how's Raju today?

Raju: I am fine uncle... (pause) Oh, yes... did you work out your speech today on world peace? And how to get rid of dangerous weapons?

John: (resigned) Yes, but I know what they will say... as long as there is fear among people, everyone needs to arm and protect themselves. (John gestures everyone to join the table; conversation continues while they make their way to the table)

Raju: (cheering up) Uncle, do you know what Swami Vivekananda said? He said... "what brings fear in our hearts is the only evil that exists".

Vicki: (eye gesture at Misha) That's why I am not afraid of big sister anymore.

Misha: (threatening gesture) oh, really? We will talk about it later, OK? (Vicki looks scared)

Gauri: (conciliatory) Let's not talk about evil and weapons this lovely morning.

Vicki: (still looking at Misha) Mom! I think some people are more frightening than weapons. (Misha gives a dirty look)

Raju: If you carry on like this, I will not teach you to play flute... I will take it back from you.

Vicki: Sorry, Raju! I think it's better to learn flute than to fight with didi.

John: OK, let's attack food now. (by now everyone is seated around the table and begins eating; after a few seconds, John stops pensively, rural sounds followed by Raga effect on Piano; turns to Gauri) Listen! You know it has been a while since we heard from Rangapore. (turning to Misha) Bete, why don't you drop in a letter to your grandparents?

Gauri: (reinforcing) Yeah... both Misha and Vicki should write, in Hindi, Ok? That will make Mummy and Babuji very happy. (Misha and Vicki nod)

John: (pensively) I hope... I hope one from this rat race, and live on the less of everything, and more of us. day we all can go away farm. There will be Anyway... (Raga effect on piano ends; turning to Misha) And how's school Bete?

Misha: We are doing a project on Indian history and <u>government</u>.

Raju: Now, that's a great subject, isn't it?

Misha: And, we have to make presentations today. That makes me a little nervous.

John: I see, but what are you going to present?

Misha: (methodically) I am going to talk about ancient literature and the birth of modern science. What I couldn't figure out is how to deal with human gods... so many of them. Any ideas?

Raju: How about dealing with just one god... your own god... your witness!

Misha: Well... I don't know who or what is my god. Mom could you please pass me a toast. Let me first fill my stomach, then I will think about my god.

Raju: Auntie, may I have some butter please, my favorite food.

(Gauri is serving everybody. Vicki shows his pinky and leaves for bathroom. After a few minutes breakfast is over. Everyone gets up, and into departure routine clearing table, packing school bag, putting on shoes, combing hair, stopping near the mirror, etc. Some comic situations as they rush, get into others' way, drop and pick up things, try to be cool. The following conversation intermingles with departure routine)

Gauri: OK, it's time to get ready for school.

John: (putting on his tie and jacket, turning to Misha) Bete, why don't you take Raju to your school today? I think it will be fun for him to visit an American school. And you are having this interesting project on India. How about that Raju, would you like to go? I think you will have fun.

Raju: Sure, uncle... (hesitates) But please tell didi not to leave me alone. I don't know how to talk in American accent.

John: Don't worry, Raju... Misha will take care of you. Won't you bete?

Misha: Yes, but Raju, you will have to dress up nicely.

Raju: (nods) for me? OK... could you please choose the right clothes for me?

Misha: Just get an older and dirtier shirt. (pause, laugh) Actually, what you are wearing is fine. Just comb your hair and put on your shoes.

Raju: (exits to get ready) OK, I will be back in a minute.

(School bus horns outside. Vicki comes in running)

Vicki: My bus is here... bye!

(Vicki kisses everyone; they wish him "have a nice day". Others are almost ready to leave)

Misha: Come on Raju, we better get going too. (cajoling) Mom, let me drive your car today, please. Then, you wouldn't have to worry about driving to school. You can finish your breakfast... slowly, and make a nice dinner for us. Since you are starting your job next week, this week you need to take it easy... right?

Gauri: (concerned) OK... but drive carefully. Roads are getting more crowded, and drivers are getting more Impatient.

Misha: Mom, don't worry about that. (comes close to avoid being heard by John) Mom, can I go to the mall after school. (Gauri hesitates and gestures negative) But other kids go to the mall all the time.

Gauri: No, not today. No trip to the mall today. You forgot, we have invited some people over this evening. And I will need your help.

John: (watching to eavesdrop, comes close) Your mother is right, we need you at home

<u>Gauri:</u> (firmly) And besides, you don't need to do everything that others do. (Misha looks irritated and disappointed)

<u>John:</u> (moves close to Misha) And listen... sometimes let your friends want to be like you, rather than you always wanting to be like them. Remember... it's OK to be different... sometimes... for a reason. (Misha nods, smiles)

<u>Gauri:</u> (changing subject) And do you know why I am starting that job next week, the job I really don't want or need?.. Partly to stay away from those useless afternoon tea parties at the Congressional Wives Club... but mainly to save money for your college next year.

<u>Misha:</u> (chuckles) but the other day you said you want to save for my wedding. And another day, you said you want to save for our trip to India in December... and you want to have enough money to go crazy in Karol Bagh.

<u>Gauri:</u> (retorts) don't knock India and Karol Bagh. I hear things are getting better there. Everything is now available... Coke, KFC, Kellogg cereals, Karaoke tapes, everything.

<u>John:</u> (reluctantly to Gauri) and that's why you are going to torture yourself sitting in the office at you new job? (jokingly to Misha) You really want to know the truth, bete? Your mom wants to buy a new dining set she saw at Nieman Marcus.

Misha: (sees mom upset; quietly exits, calling) Raju, let's go now... I don't want to be late.

Gauri: (complaining to John) Stop teasing me like that, in front of the kids.

John: Why? That's the truth, isn't it? Anyway, look, I am sorry... OK?

Gauri: (lecture mode) You Indian men... always put down your women... and expect them to stay quiet... before you accuse them of talking too much.

(Misha and Raju return, wish goodbye and depart for school. John and Gauri change tone, and look normal temporarily to send them off)

John: (to Misha) And listen... your question about god?... on your way to school, talk it over with Raju, OK?

Misha: OK, dad... bye... take care.

(Kids are gone. John approaches Gauri to apologies.)

John: (apology) Honey, again... I am sorry. I shouldn't have said all that.

Gauri: (returns to her angry mood) So what if I want to buy a new dining set. Ot Otherwise, when people come to our house, they will say that nothing has improved since you became Senator. We have to live according to your status, your power... (smiles) and my taste.

John: (serious) You know, sometimes I feel that the real power is in the words that Raju speaks. (looks at Gauri, changes tone) And, of course, in the words that you speak.

Gauri: (pretending) Will you stop teasing me... again?

John: (naughtily romantic) OK... I will stop teasing you... - and start loving you.. again. How about right now... (tries to kiss Gauri, she wiggles out and escapes)

Gauri: No... not now... please... I promise... tonight... ("Somewhere my love" instrumental on soundtrack begins)

John: (holding Gauri's hands; happiness combined with melancholy)) Aren't we lucky to have such a happy family. Now with Raju, our family seens more complete... (looks at his watch, gets ready to leave; business-like tone) I better get going too. There is an important hearing on the Hill today; it's about foreign trade, which means sanctions against the Japanese- can't live with them, can't live without them.

Gauri: Those people on the Hill need less hearing... and more listening... everything will work out better then...

John: (naughty tone) Just like I always listen to you. (laughs, comes close and hugs gauri) I hope, I hope you won't forget your promise... (Gauri blushes) tonight... right?

Gauri: (hiding joy) oh, for that... you will have to remind me. (They laugh, John departs; instrumental piece ends)

(Gauri now left alone, cleans breakfast table. Smiles, hums, and mumbles to herself. Plays a music tape- "Babul mora naihar chhooto ri jaye" Goes to stop the tape, but starts it again. One full stanza on soundtrack. Or a Thumri (Sajan dekho aayi hai bahar or Abhi to main jawan hoon) could be played through the change of set) Light dims with spot on Gauri. She sits down, closes her eyes. Music continues, then fades out. Lights fade out. End of scene. Duration 15-20 mins. Curtain remains open. Stage light dims to change props and prepare for the classroom scene)

———•♦•———

ACT-2: SCENE-2

(History classroom. Comic fusion music begins. Casual atmosphere. Students milling around, joking, some roughness. Atmosphere changes when Misha and Raju enter. A few students are talking; girls are busy with themselves- one is preparing flip-charts. India project presentations about to begin.)

Charlie: (chewing ice from cup) Hey guys, did anyone do the homework?

Mike: Homework? My foot. I don't even know where India is. I couldn't find it on the US map. I even found Rhode Island, but couldn't find India. (laughs, munching chips) Man... what a topic for class presentation! (points to flip- charts) Hey, Tina... do you know where India is?

Tina: It's on the first chart... with a big north and a small south... just like your face. (everyone laughs)

Carl: (putting his foot down from chair) Maybe, today we will learn something from Misha- the Indian girl...

charlie yeah the only Indian girl in the class who is not an American. It will be fun... can't wait.

Mike: Misha... and fun? You must be kidding. She is so weird, so square, so different, but so cute. And you know what she says... "it's ok to be different, for a reason". Man... I tell ya.

Charlie: I know what you mean... all geeks are like that.

Mary: That's why you are not one... but secretly wish you were.

Julia: (childish expression) And poor Mike... cou couldn't find India on the US map... What a loser! First, why don't you try to find USA on the world map?

Mike: (aggravated) Look, I don't want no trouble... I don't want to know what I don't need to... Now, tell me... do you know where Timbaktu is? I bet you don't. I don't know either... and I don't care.

Carl: Hey, watch out. There she is... with a bodyguard... eh!

(Misha and Raju enter Flute music piece. They quietly take back seats, and settle down.)

Charlie: Look, what we got here... Misha- the babysitter...

Misha: Shut up... he is like my brother, my baby brother.

Charlie: Poor baby... cute boy... like his sister (laughs) Bennett enters.

Mr. Bennett: (cheerful) Good morning everybody! (turning to Raju, expression changes) Hi, who are you? Something wrong with you?

Raju: (embarrassed) No, sir. My name is Rajesh Nandan Parthasarathy, sir.

Chorus: Whaaaat? (giggles)

Mike: Could you say that again? Is that your name? or... your autobiography? (class giggles, Mr. Bennett brings order)

Raju: Please forget my long name… just call me Raju.

Mr. Bennett: Raju... hmm... why are you standing, Raju?

Raju: Sir, I am used to standing up when the teacher comes in the classroom, as a sign of respect, sir. (everyone giggles)

Mr. Bennett: (Jokingly) Alright, that's very nice. Well... I... I don't know how to deal with a student who respects the teacher. Anyway, please sit down. Are you a new student at the school?

Misha: (explaining) Mr. Bennett, Raju is my house guest. He is visiting us from India this summer. I thought he might be bored sitting at home, and we were doing our India project, so I asked him to come with me to the class. I hope you don't mind.

Mr. Bennett: (hiding joy) No, no, that's alright. It's a pleasure to have a nice young man like Raju join the class today. Before we begin our individual presentations, maybe we can ask you, Raju, to say something about yourself.

Raju: (in flat prose) Sir, I am 14 years old. I was born in India. I am a 9th class student at Krishna High School in Mathura near New Delhi. My summer vacation has already started. I will be staying with Senator Pandey's family for two months. Then I will go back home. I have one brother. My parents and everybody in my village love me very much. Thank you, sir. (smiles)

Mr. Bennett: That's nice... OK, now let's start with our presentations on Indian history and governpunchment.

Raju: (half-standing then sits down) Excuse me, sir. What is governpunchment?

Mr. Bennett: You see, government is such a boring subject. We wanted to put some punch in it. (shows punching motion) we call it govern- punch-ment. (everyone laughs) OK, OK, let's have a quiz on your reading assignment. What is the main role of government?

(No response) Come on, what does the government do? OK, what's the government supposed to do?

(Different students raise hands, and talk when acknowledged by Mr. Bennett. Some over-enthusiasm.)

Carl: I think the government's job is to... annoy people (laugh) Come

Mr. Bennett: Come on, please be serious.

Mary: Help those who can't help themselves.

Mr. Bennett: Hm... That's better.

Tina: Ensure our safety and <u>freedom</u>, and worry about future generations.

Mr. Bennett: Good... Anybody else wants to take a shot?

Raju: What... take a shot at the government?

Mr. Bennett: No, by that I mean... make another guess.

Raju: I have no guess. But I have a question, sir.

Mr. Bennett: OK, go right ahead... shoot.

Raju: If the government does all these things, then what is the problem, sir?

Joe: You see... the government is used to not doing it's job... and people are used to not worrying about it. Everybody is happy, aren't we? No problem, except...

Mr. Bennett: You guys are real sharp today... Now let's ask Raju... How does the government work in India?

Raju: (innocently) Sir, I have not seen the government in India or in America. I only hear people talk about it. And I find it very confusing, sir.

Mr. Bennett: (pointedly) I don't blame you. I have read about other kinds of confusion in India too. You have a caste system; people burn baby girls and brides; there is lot of corruption... and politicians are the biggest...

Raju: (agitated) You are right, sir. (serious tone) But I am telling you... I am going to stop all that... not me alone, everybody who loves me, is going to stop that.

Mr. Bennett: (in disbelief) My, my, Raju. You are going to do all that? Maybe we need a Raju here in America too. When you go back, please try and find an extra Raju for us. Would' ya?

Misha: (tough pretense) Raju, aren't we talking too much today?

Raju: (smiles) Sorry... (puts his hand to shut his mouth)

Mr. Bennett: OK, Misha! Would you like to present your project now? Why don't you go first.

Misha: (goes to front of class, refers to index cards;) I did a report on the Vedic literature and the birth of modern science... including creation of the physical universe...

Tina: But we've already read about the origin... don't you know the big bang theory?

Misha: (dismiss) Well... big bang is more like an attitude. As a theory, it is difficult to prove with the science we know today. Let's not forget there are some other ideas too... OK... let me begin/Temphatically) The word Veda means eternal knowledge, as perceived by the ancient Rishis of India. Rishi means the knower. The Vedic knowledge existed always, but was visualized in the consciousness of the Rishis.

Tina: Wait a minute that sounds too mystical.

Misha: Only if you are too skeptical... OK, let me continue. There are 4 main Vedas: Rigveda, Yajurveda, Samveda and Atharvaveda. There are no records as to when the Vedas were written, or who the authors were. These texts were interpreted.

Raju: (hesitates to interrupt) Didi, you forgot to mention the Upavedas such as Gandharvaveda for music, Ayurveda for perfect health, Sthapatyaveda for architecture...

Misha: (dislikes Raju's interruption; cuts him short) Thank you Raju. OK... the Vedas were further elaborated and interpreted by many Rishis, and explained to their students. Those detailed dialogues between the teachers and the students are recorded in what is called the Upanishads. And there are over a hundred Upanishads. All this knowledge was simplified for the common people in the form of mythological stories. These are called the Puranas. (pause) The great epics- Ramayan and Mahabharat on the other hand...

Charlie: (purposely interrupts) And where do the thousands of Indian gods come from?

Misha: (annoyed) Hey Charlie, don't interrupt. (Mr. Bennett gestures Charlie to behave; Misha regains composure) OK... those gods were imagined by people to represent the forces of nature, or anything people thought was higher than themselves. The ancient texts talk about just one god, who can appear to be different, and there are many paths to reach him. And that one god is supposed to be the ultimate knowledge or intelligence, and source of energy which creates the material universe, and keeps it going.

Mr Bennett: But that is how we interpret god in Christianity.

Joe: And... Allah Al-Noor... the same in Islam. Then what is so different with Indian god?

Misha: Joey, that's what I am trying to say... there's no difference. It is the same god, only we think differently.

Mr. Bennett: Hm... That's very interesting Misha... Let's now try to wrap up now.

Mike: Yeah... and also tell us about the snake-charmers, elephants and cows.

Misha: Holy cow, Mike, those things you can read in the newspapers. I am now going to talk about the birth of modern science in the Vedic litereture. This will cover the main ideas of mathematics, physics, and creation of matter. In the end, I will talk about GUTs thrown up by the Vedas.

Mike: Ugh... that sounds nasty. I hope you are not serious... about throwing up guts.

(Raju gets up impatiently, speaks with supernatural force; everyone is stunned)

Raju: Didi Before that, let's explain some of the main ideas in the Vedas... That everything is cyclical, reborn nothing gets destroyed... something like the law of conservation of energy. What changes is material... what remains permanent is divine. That action produces reaction- the law of Karma- which is like Newton's Third law. That creation exists in layers... each layer is a universe? like the solar system from far would look like an atom. That all knowledge resides in our consciousness. We- the knower- must go higher and deeper to become one with the knowledge. Unless that happens, we will only know a part of the truth... like the uncertainty principle. By knowing ourselves perfectly, will know everything else... Like the whole knowledge of the tree is hidden in the seed. But to understand that first we must learn to lower the frequency of Alpha rays in our brains. That all forces of nature become one at a point we can feel only but cannot explain... let's call it sub-quantum mechanics...

(Raju now notices everyone's gaze, realizes he overspoke, retreats to child-like mannerism, stops, closes his eyes, and sits down, pause)

Misha: (breaking silence, slightly irritated) Raju! Is this my presentation or yours'?

Mr. Bennett: Actually that was quite in the way you explained ancient knowledge in terms of modern science.

(Everyone still awestruck, looking at Raju; Misha tries to draw attention, more gently) Raju! You made my job easier. Now I can go back and make my final point... GUT in physics stands for "grand unification theory"... a single theory which can unify and explain the four main forces of nature: gravity, electromagnetism, strong nuclear force, and weak nuclear force...

(Everyone still amazed: "vow, that sounds interesting" "Can't wait" "Man, that's cool" "can't believe it", etc. Suddenly, all voices are drowned by the sound of gun-shots. Chaos both on soundtrack and in classroom. Running, screaming, hiding, etc. Lights slowly dims to dark)

Mr. Bennett: (in panic) Hey... let's move out of here... quick. On your knees... everybody... don't panic... crawl out... not this way... over there... watch out...

(All students leave stage and run through the audience, and exit through the entrance door. Misha is heard saying "Raju, are you alright?" Raju calmly gets up, exits left stage, brushing debri from his arms. Silence... after 10 seconds, curtain begins to close. At the same time, Mr. Bennett returns in front of curtain hurriedly, than stops, looks exhausted.)

Mr. Bennett: (explaining to the audience, poundingly) Ladies and gentlemen! There was a disturbance on school campus. Sorry about the inconvenience. Unfortunately, we are going to miss the remainder of Misha's very interesting presentation... because we can't go back to the classroom right now... it's in total mess. But never mind, everything will be fine... (pauses, smiles, then back to normal tone) You know something! This may be a good time to break for intermission. But don't worry, it's perfectly safe to go the bathroom, and have snacks in the lobby. (exits running)

(Lights dim to off. Manthan music begins. Curtain remains closed. End of scene. Duration 20 mins. Stage to be rearranged for Senator's living room.)

———◆◆———

Intermission

ACT-3: SCENE-1

(Evening time in Senator's living room. Vocal overture for flute piece. Dim lights. Raju is sitting alone, begins playing flute- live coordination with soundtrack. Shiny make-up on face and hair. After two minutes, he puts his flute away and sits down with his eyes closed in meditative pose. There is a glowing golden halo around him. John walks in, puts his briefcase away, looks at Raju, observes, remains quiet, sits down near Raju, the halo expands to cover him. After 10 seconds, Raju slowly opens his eyes, halo disappears, notices John, smiles, closes his eyes again, slowly normalizes. Abridged ACT-3 is 30 minutes; expanded version, with an additional scene, is 55 minutes. For abridged version, skip pages 53-62)

John: (concerned) Are you not feeling well, Raju?

Raju: (calmly) everything will be fine uncle. How was your day?

John: (disgusted, gets up) Oh, as usual... party politics, lobby groups, endless discussions, too many problems, not enough solutions... how to spend the money we don't have, to solve the problems which don't need money. Everybody trying to second guess everyone else. (Pathetic) It's becoming a drag, Raju. I feel tired... how long will I have to continue like this...

<u>Raju:</u> (starry, has gotten up by now) Why don't you do something different, uncle?

<u>John:</u> (resigned look) But, everyone wants to talk, nobody wants to listen. Gets up

<u>John:</u> (closes his eyes) You are talking about godly things, Raju. These days, many people don't believe in these things.

<u>Raju:</u> (emphatically, and quickly) They will... believe me Uncle, they will. Remember, they are the same as you... one with nature, one with god. Just ask them to imagine the sun, look at a flower, see the picture of that broken comet crashing into Jupiter, and... then feel their own pulse.

<u>John:</u> (ambivalent) Then, I should have done that in the Senate today. But who has got the time for these things. Listen Raju! Sometimes I feel I am just talking to myself. And why should they listen to me? They don't regard me as an American... they think I am still very Indian. And my Indian friends think I am too Americanized. That makes it difficult to convince anybody. I don't have the right image. My reality is different, Raju.

Raju: (meaningful gaze) Uncle, I remember the words of my Guruji reality is one... yours is no different from mine, or theirs'. And the images... they are creations of individual minds. And the further those minds are from truth... from reality, the further apart those images are. Believe in your ideas and your actions, Uncle.

John: (throws up hands) But how would I know if my ideas and actions are the right ones?

Raju: (pointedly) By just making sure that your own goals... your personal goals... don't clash with what is good for other people, and don't hurt mother nature.

John: I can't imagine... a perfect man... any man, who could always be doing the right thing.

Raju: Just imagine yourself... or someone, who can feel the pain of a hungry mother... a lonely child; or who can feel happier by giving than by having; or who can treat the flower and the river like his car and VCR...

John: Raju, I still don't understand fully... tell me. How would I know what is good for everybody? what is good for mother nature? What is the true nature of things?

Raju: Uncle, you know the answer... within yourself... everyone does. Just clear your mind of random thoughts and frustrations, and ask yourself. If you still don't find the answer, take a walk along the river, in the morning, when the water is calm... and the trees are quiet...

John: (bursts) Raju, the way you speak... everything sounds so simple, but isn't so. Just tell me... how do I clear my mind of random thoughts?...

(Music piece drowns their voices, but their silent conversation continues. Raju clarifies, John understands. Then music fades low while noises of Gauri and Misha overheard. John and Raju discontinue their conversation, and start to tidy up the living room.)

Raju: (hush) I think Auntie and Didi are here.

John: (hush) Very well, we will continue our conversation later... I need to do that. I am now beginning to understand.

(Gauri and Misha enter. Exchange of pleasantries)

Gauri: (happily, to John) I am glad to see you at home early today. (Turning to Raju) I am sure your uncle came home early so he can talk with you more. (Changing tone) That's the only reason. (To John) I know, you wouldn't make time for me and the kids.

John: (sadly) Darling! Please don't misunderstand.

Gauri: (confrontational) don't worry, I am now beginning to understand you... what really matters to you. You are looking just for your own happiness... you don't really care for us. Do you know what happened at Misha's school today?

(Raju is quiet and smiling. John is pensive and unresponsive, and mentally retreats away to his prior chat with Raju.)

Misha: (mumbling) I still can't get over what happened at school today. Those stupid gun-shots... ruined the best part of my presentation. What a loss! Dad, didn't Raju tell you anything about it?

John: (lost in thoughts, feeling an enjoyable spell; as if answering a different question) Yes, Bete... Raju told me a lot of things. There is a path... there is a way. Now, I think I can find it... I must. Everything will happen in time. (pauses; changes expression) oh, those gun-shots... yes... don't worry... there are people who have suffered greater loss due to crime. One day... I hope... we all will be from violence.

(Raju begins to leave the stage, with a meaningful smiling face. Vicki is entering. Raju hugs Vicki, goes to pick up 7 his flute, and hands it over to Vicki before departing. Vicki makes a sad goodbye gesture to Raju.)

Vicki: (first looks serious, then changes expression) 1-2-3... Daddy is free. 2-3-4... Raju no more. (Repeats in serious tone and slow tempo)

John: (upset) Vicki! What did you say? Raju no more? What do you mean?

(Vicki looks scared; goes hides near Gauri)

Gauri: Why are you getting so upset? You know, Raju will have to return to India one day. What will you do then?

John: We shall see, when that time comes.

(Now light dims to dark. Jazz music piece on soundtrack. Drop spots at center stage appear intermittently to show John, Gauri, Misha and Vicki in 5-6 different frozen motions. The idea here is to show passage of time. In the last couple of spots, John is missing. Pause. No light or sound. Soft music fades in and out. Pause. Windstorm combined with chimes fades in and out. Pause. Red drop spot appears on John sitting in chair in napping posture, dressed in white shirt and black pants. Picture appears on screen, both in long and medium shots, without sound, showing a few clips of John in the foreground of Capitol Hill, followed by a casual silent conversation after his unexpected encounter with Debby. Picture blurs. Five seconds pause. John wakes up appears drowsy, searching for something. Debby dressed in Kathak style costumes and ghungru walks in to center stage, turning and pointing toward John. Blue drop spot appears on Debby. John and Debby are in slow-motion conversational posture.

NOTE: there is no indication that John and Debby are having a relationship. This scene only reflects the impact each has made on the other's subconscious mind. The following romantic dialogues are heard from soundtrack.)

Debby: (softly) How are you feeling John? I see you look tired. I am sorry, if I give you hard time.

John: (tired voice) Oh Debby! I am Ok... just thinking about you... why? I don't know.

Debby: (jovial) I was thinking about you too... and I do know why... John! I am proud of you, your dedication, your commitment, your compassion, your love...

John: (emphasis) Debby! I want to thank you for keeping me alert... on track. You have such a clear mind. I like how you cut through the fog, and get to the point, so easily... how you can read people's minds through their words. I wish there were more women like you, Debby.

Debby: (whisper) And I wish, there were more men like you, John. at least one more... you know why?...

(Suspense music in night Raga fades in, drowns the above conversation, and fades out. Drop spot and Debby disappear. Spot remains on John who is now changing postures. Selected utterances by Raju are now heard on pre-recorded soundtrack)

… Uncle! do you know what Swami Vivekananda said about fear? Uncle! You need to know people's thoughts, like Mahatma Gandhi did. / Then you can write that book, without words, directly in people's minds... Yes, Uncle! You can do it... / by looking deep in your mind, watching your thoughts being born. By knowing what god wants to do through you, by knowing why we are born; what is our purpose in life... By making sure that your own goals don't clash with what is good for other people, and don't hurt mother nature... / Uncle! just clear your mind of random thoughts. / One day, I will take you for a walk... along the river when the water is calm and the trees are quiet... Shh... Uncle l... listen... someone is coming... be strong... I will always be with you... always.

(Quiet. Fog Then Stanley enters stage to his music piece, dressed in black shirt and white pants- could add white tie and black jacket. He looks around, makes gestures at John, moves toward audience.)

Stanley: (pointing to John; facing audience in complaining mode) Look at this man! Sleeping so quietly and peacefully. Causing us so much trouble... and sleeping here like a baby. He thinks he is so special... custom-made by some god in India... sent here to solve our problems in America. But you know something! He is not solving anything, just asking too many questions... trying to make us think differently... wants to change everything, Ha. / You know what I think? I think he has got it made... too good, here in America. And now he is in business of finding faults in other people. He wants to prove us wrong. But I tell you, we won't let that happen in a 100 years.

(Light dims on Stanley, then resumes after Debby appears on big screen, reporting. Stanley pauses to watch)

Debby: (on screen; reporting mode) In a 100 years, we haven't heard such a short and simple State-of-the-union address by any president. The speech tonight by President Burt Greenwich can be summed up in just four sentences: The state-of-the-union is just fine; There will be cuts in taxes and social security; The Department of Justice will merge with the Human Rights Commission; and a new Department of Public Relations will be created, to allow people to send in their complaints through the Internet. (pause) I will be back in a moment with comments by Arjun Pandey- the Independent Senator from the State of Maryland. (finally, Debby pronounces the name correctly)

Stanley: (claps and the picture disappears; he continues; to audience) Sounds good You see! That's the kind of change we need. We live in a free and prosperous society / And this man- John, our beloved Senator- wants to slow down our progress, save the rats and the birds, close down our arms and defense industries, dismantle our education system, and have everybody sit and wait with their eyes closed. / Too bad, he doesn't belong to a political party, otherwise, they would have checked and fixed him already.

(Meanwhile, John has risen suddenly and moved toward Stanley. John recognizes Stanley. Stanley changes his expression to appear respectful.)

John: (pleading) Stanley! Please don't misunderstand me. I don't want people to sit with their eyes closed. I want them to open their eyes to our problems... and build an even more prosperous society. Because, I believe, America hasn't seen it's best days yet. (pauses, remembers) By the way, I thought we went through this discussion on the Hill today. Who are you lobbying for now? What are you selling now?

Stanley: We want to sell more of everything... guns, butter, cars, radars, anything... anything that makes money... now.

John: Anything? Are you sure?

Stanley: (proudly) Well, yes... we are a free society. Let people decide what they want to have, what they want to do. (pause) I can't understand you Senator! On one hand, you speak of this land as the envy of all people; on the other hand, you say things are not fine here.

Why don't you make up your mind first? Why can't you see things the way I do?

John: (with confidence) Stanley! I did make up my mind... before I plunged into politics. You see, my only question is... are we really making the right choices?... Are we really making the best use of our <u>freedom</u>?

Stanley: (sarcastically) So, now you will tell us what is right for us, what is good for us. Who do you think you are? A prophet or something?... (pause, then firm voice) We won't let you mess with our <u>freedom</u>, Senator... remember that...

(Meanwhile, a double-masked man #1 enters stage to his music piece, through fog. Audience sees one side. Pauses near John. John is dazed)

#1: You were just remembering me.

John: Who are you?

 # 1: I am <u>freedom</u>.

John: But why do you have two faces?

#1: (turns around) One for you, and... One for him... (Pointing to Stanley).

Stanley: Boy! Is that confusing? I am going home (he leaves, saying:) Senator! I will see you later, on the Hill.

(Another double-masked man enters stage to his music piece, through fog)

John: And who are you?

#2: I am <u>government</u>. This side for you, and... (turning around) this side for everyone else.

John: But why two sides?

#2: You see, after all... we are humans... all the same, but all so different

(A third double-masked man enters stage to his music piece, through fog)

#3: Ha-ha-ha... and now you will ask... who am I? (pause) I am democracy. People love me but they haven't yet figured out how to deal with me. See... my one hand is hot, and... the other cold.

(Note: These masked persons have one identical mask on one side, and different ones on the other. Each has different style, mannerism, and unnatural voice. They all are draped in black. John now looks anguished and sweaty. Then #4 without mask enters to his music piece, through fog- this one appears faceless.)

#4: And you would never know who I am. Try to guess. (John looks puzzled) I am justice. Nobody knows how I look.

John: May I ask... why are you all here? What have I done?

#1: You have questioned me.

#2: You have annoyed me.

#3: You have disturbed me.

#4: And you have doubted my existence.

All Four in unison: We have to teach you a lesson... you will never forget.

(They begin to overpower John. Minor struggle ensues. John has been pushed to sit in his original chair and posture.)

John: Please... help... Oh God...

(Vicki enters stage slowly, but rushes to John, and begins to resist the four intruders.)

Vicki: Dad!... (to intruders) please... please leave my dad alone. (starts crying)

#4: OK, boy, alright. We will leave your dad alone... And take you away with us... Then he will be really left alone. Come on... let's go...

(Now all four drag and kidnap Vicki; and begin to leave stage. Struggle continues)

John: No... please... no. What has this boy done to you? (tries but cannot get up from his chair... cries out loud) No... please don't take my son away... help... Oh God!

(John remains in panic while others leave stage. Gauri enters hurriedly as if overhearing John. She is surprised to see John's condition, approaches him lovingly.)

Gauri: Darling! What has happened to you? Who was here? Why are you sweating?

John: (recomposes himself, gets up) Oh... nothing... really. It must have been a bad dream... but seemed so real... And where is Vicki?

Gauri: Darling! Vicki is fine. He is watching TV with Misha. (pause) But what are you doing here... alone... lost in thoughts... again?

John: (withdrawn) No, I don't want to be lost in thoughts anymore... They are becoming more and more scary.

Gauri: But why do you have unpleasant thoughts to begin with? Look... you have all the good things going for you... nice family... good money... high status, prestige... everything.

John: (sigh) You are right... I have everything... except one... (Gauri looks puzzled)... happiness. Raju used to say- real happiness is permanent, but first I have to stop struggling...

NOTE: This scene is to be included in the expanded (full-length) version of this play. For the abridged version, SKIP pages 55-64)

(Noises of Gauri and Anju being overheard in reference to the party tonight. John and Raju discontinue their conversation and begin to tidy up the living room.)

Anju: Mom, how do you like my outfit.

Gauri: Very pretty... I am glad you are not wearing jeans and t- shirt for the party. Now, help me choose a saree.

Anju: Sure, nom. Sarees are so misleading... look so simple... and so delicate... but so hard to put it on properly.

Gauri: (louder) Vicki... Vicki... (Vicki responds) please go to the kitchen, and see if I left the stove on.

Vicki: OK, mom. (running sound) Mom... guess what... dad is home already, and we didn't know. I saw his car in the garage.

Gauri: I am so glad he is home early today, for a change. At least he didn't forget about the party tonight.

Raju: (overhearing outside conversation) I think auntie and didi are here.

John: Very well, we will continue our conversation later... I need to do that. I need to understand.

(Gauri and Anju enter. Exchange of pleasantries)

Gauri: I am glad to see you at home early today. (turning to Raju) I am sure your uncle came home early so he can talk to you more.

Raju: No... auntie, he came early to help you prepare for the party.

John: (hesitatingly) Yes... darling, Raju is right.

Anju: (sarcastically) Mom, I know dad is really going to help you. Let me rearrange this room, just tell me what to do.

Gauri: Set the table for dinner, bring in more chairs from the kitchen, and listen... bring the big pillows from the basement, some people would end up sitting on the floor for the music session. And get some new tapes... of old songs.

John: And don't forget my favorite CD- "Ravi Shankar inside the Kremlin"

Gauri: (turning to Vicki) And Vicki bete, please remove your books and toys from this room.

(everybody now helps rearrange the props)

John: Boss, now tell me what to do... Raju will help me too.

Gauri: Why don't you guys take charge of drinks and the sound system.

(John and Raju arrange glasses, napkins, ice, microphones, instruments, etc. Vicki cleans up trash. Gauri and Anju arrange snacks. Meanwhile...)

Gauri: Have you invited any of your friend from the capital hill?

John: No I didn't. They might think I am too ethnic. indian people... Indian food... Indian music. I am already having some problem because of that, you know.

Gauri: Maybe, we can invite them later, separately. But tonight, we will have Indian style party. I have the food catered by Bukhara restaurant; dressed in our Indian clothes, we will play Indian music, talk about Indian movies. It will be fun, wouldn't it?.

John: You didn't tell me who all are coming tonight.

Gauri: You know, I have noticed lately... nobody declines our invitation. I have asked... (guest list) And, of course, Mitali is coming; she has such a sweet voice, just a little show off. I can't wait to listen to her singing. Babul will play tabla and Rohit will play guitar.

Anju: Mom, you forgot about Debby Perkins... she is so tough but so sweet. And my history teacher Chris and his wife Joan, they are coming too. (mumbles) I still can't get over what happened at school today. Those stupid gunshots... ruined the best part of my presentation.

Gauri: Never mind. Just be on your guard wherever you go. In today's society, nobody is safe... anywhere.

John: Your mother is right, bete... (turning to Gauri) And make sure tonight, you don't start the 3-S discussion.

Gauri: And what is 3-S?

John: Sale, sarees, and Shahrukh Khan.

Gauri: Why Shahrukh Khan?

John: Aren't you obsessed by him since you watched Maya Memsahib?

Gauri: (upset) What do you think I am... always trying to put me down. You know, I don't appreciate it. (goes and sits down on sofa)

Vicki: (stops what he is doing) Why is there always a fight, everytime we are going to have a party?

John: (goes to Gauri) Darling, I am sorry. I didn't mean to upset you. (holds her hand to pull up) Look, what the kids are going to think. And besides, you look better smiling.

Gauri: (gets up, smiles) OK, I forgive you... again. Help the kids, finish your work. I will check the mirror and be back soon.

Raju: (testing microphones) Hello, 1-2-3, uncle is free; 2-3-4, Raju no more

Anju: What do you mean, Raju no more?

Raju: Well... I mean, one day I will have to go back.

John: Let's have fun tonight. Don't even think about going back... we will talk about it later.

(Anju plays a music tape- selected filmi instrumentals- with subliminal messages. guests begin to arrive. Greetings. Small talk. Some are standing, some in chairs. Drinks and snacks being served. Gauri enters later, another round of greetings. Anju is offering samosas, Raju is also helping. Ladies admiring Gauri's saree. Cocktail conversation ensues. Men attentive to John, and reluctantly to Gauri. Add or modify dialogues based on the nature and availability of cast.)

Mitali: Oh, samosas? Lovely. I just had some... in the lobby. This looks good. Just give me two. I am still on diet, you know.

(Later gauri calls in Vicki to bring mango and guava juice; Anju and Raju offer to serve.)

Amit: Mitali, I hope you are going to sing tonight.

Mitali: Oh, I don't know... ay voice has gone flat, after all that chutney... not good for throat, you know.

Shankar: (attentive to taped music- "Kahena hi kya") Bhai what a lovely song from "Bombay", my favorite movie.

Amit: My favorite movie is "Garam Hawa". What a powerful film, yaar.

Monica: Looks like religious riots is a popular subject with you guys.

Chris: What is the meaning of "Garam Hawa"?

Monica: Hot... hm (stops)

Rajan: You know when the air becomes warm suit as in summer... Anyway (turning to Gopal and Rakesh) What is your favorite movie?

Gopal: "Hum Apke Hain Kaun"

Rakesh: "Khalnayak"

Amit: I see. I can guess what is your favorite subject... Madhuri Dixit... I don't blame you.

Gauri: Did you see "Anjaam"? Shahrukh baby really looks cute in there. And all the horrible things that Madhuri does, I don't like that... Let's change the topic now. Poor Joan is getting bored.

Joan: That's alright. Maybe when I see the film, I will understand what you mean. But I wonder what Indian people think about American films.

Gopal: oh, they don't think; they just like to watch. (laugh)

Geeta: (to Debby) Hi Debby... I like your show. I like when you give hard time to those rich and famous guys. But I think you need to handle John a bit more gently.

Debby: Actually, my bosses want more controversy, more exceptions, more sensations. That's what makes the news. I don't really like that too much. Maybe I should change my profession.

John: Debby, come on... I would rather be interviewed by you than anyone else. You make people think.

Rakesh: This is getting too intellectual now. (turning to Gopal) How was your trip to India?

Gopal: Lovely... lots of people, dirty politics, but I love the country.

Amit: I heard now you can get Coke, Kellogs cereal, and Karoake tapes in India. That's real progress. Even the kids now feel quite at home in India.

Gopal: Provided they don't eat golgappas on the street and get diarhea. (laugh) Or be tempted to ride the 4-wheeler and get bronchitis.

(Reggie enters in suit and dark glasses)

John: Hello there! You are late again, as usual. (turning to others)

Here's our good friend... Reg in English... Rajiv in Hindi. Just like I am John in English and Arjun in Hindi. In his hometown Hyderabad, he is known as the pop singer from America. (everyone says hello, etc)

Reg: Sorry, I an late. I was stuck in auditioning for a play. They made me read the role three times... then offered it to someone else. Too bad... they will miss me.

John: Never mind... have a drink... you will be OK. (turning to Joan) How's Chris treating you these days?

Joan: He just loves his job, teaching history, living in the past.

Chris: Come on, I am interested in the present too. Senator, What's happening in the Congress these days?

Joan: I heard they are always overworked, underpaid, undermined, and under investigation. (laugh)

John: (in Gauris ears, jokingly) You see? That's why I didn't want to invite anybody from the Hill.

Joan: Senator, i am sorry... that joke wasn't mine. I read it in the latest edition of truly tasteless jokes"

Reg: I must say that tasteless jokes in America are at least more practical than in India.

Gauri: Let's cut out all the tasteless jokes, hear some music. (to Anju) Anju bete, please turn off the tape music.

(Everyone agrees. Sound system is already set up. Position microphones. Connect keyboard. Set up and tune tabla. Some sit, some stand. Rohit plays Lada- the theme song from Dr. Zhivago- "Somewhere my love, there will be songs to sing")

Rajan: (clapping) Lovely song... Dr. Zhivago, right? You know, I still think Dilip Kumar would have done a better job than Omar Sharif.

Monica: Well... somewhere, sometime, maybe. These words keep you guessing, keep your hopes alive. But Rohit, you are still playing this kind of song; what have you been doing until now?

Rohit: Until now, I was there. And now, I just play the tune.

John: Jokes aside, that was a lovely tune. Now let's have an English song from Reg; then a Hindi song from Mitali.

(Reg sings "when the girl in your arms is the girl in your heart". Clapping. Reg accepting complements)

Gauri: Reg, that was a very romantic song... must be an old song, right? Now Mitali, please sing a Hindi song for us.

Mitali: I told you, that chutney is bothering my throat. But if you people insist, I will sing a song, but just one, OK?

(Mitali sings "Kahan jey chaley ho; batado musafir")

Shankar: What a beautiful song...

Debby: What's the meaning of this song?

Mitali: The first line says "on which path are you taking me, O my companion; what world lies beyond the stars"?

Debby: Now, that sounds very romantic too.

Mitali: It sounds very scary to me. He may be actually taking her to wrong places, you know.

Rajni: Well, right place or wrong place depends on where you are heading to, and who is with you. But, beyond stars? I am not sure I want to go there

(More dialogues and guests can be added in this scene later for Babul, the tabla player, and other guests)

Gauri: (sees Raju helping with soda) Did you all know that Raju plays flute. Raju, won't you play a piece for us, please?

(Raju reluctantly brings his flute, goes to microphone, synchronize with playback flute and piece. Silence with dimming light. live tabla. Raju's signature People walking up to Raju. Raju seen leaving the room. End of scene. Guests leaving- rearrange props. Manthan music fades in and gets louder. Curtain close. Duration... mins)

ACT-3: SCENE-2

(In front of closed curtain, a group of people- wearing masks- walking around aimlessly. Some appear drunk, some crazy, some restless. Each one doing their own strange things. Begin with soundtrack and picture on big screen. Debby reporting):

Debby: You have just watched what can be called the President's shortest and simplest "state-of-the-Union" speech It can be summed up in four sentences. State-of-the-union is just fine. There will be lover taxes. The Department of Justice is being merged with the Human Rights Commission. And a new Public Relations Office will be created, where people can send in their complaints on 3-by-5 index cards.

(One person on stage says- "Hey, that's great". With his clap the channel changes on screen. Now Debby appears on another newscast):

Debby: (in somber tone) Senator John Pandee's family was plunged into much anxiety and uncertainty, after the Senator dreant about the kidnapping of his son Vicki

Pandee. Vicki is fine, but John is undergoing psychotherapy.

(Another person on stage says "Now, that's sickening". Pretends to throw rock, and the scene changes on screen. Now a tearful conversation between John and Gauri):

Gauri: We need to pull ourselves together. We need to think hard about how where are we going; what's happening in our lives. I wish we can go somewhere, far away from here.

John: (caressing her hair) That's what I was thinking... let's go away, with our children... to our village... to our farm... where there is less of everything... and more of us...

Gauri: I wish we could do that... but what will happen to Anju's college education from next year... I guess we will have to.

John: Let's try to bring Raju here again next summer. That will be good for Vicki too...

Gauri: And for you... I will write to Raju... but until next summer will be a long wait... (screen blurs)

(Another person on stage says- "You can wait, but I can't". Others join in- "You are right, we can't wait. Let's go...get out of here". Everybody leaves stage. Darkness and silence everywhere. Manthan music fades in. Other music pieces are superimposed intermittantly to suggest passage of time. Now it is winter time, late night. Curtain opens. Dim light on John- alone, smoking pipe.)

Gauri: (enters after 10 seconds, walks slowly to John) What are you doing here... alone... lost in thoughts.

John: No, I don't want to be lost in thoughts anymore... They are becoming more and more scary.

Gauri: soothing voice, coming close) And when will your struggles end?

John: (turning to Gauri) When I find out where Raju is.

Gauri: I miss Raju. And the kids miss him too. But, we have to be practical, and act strong. We knew, one day he had to go back where he came from.

John: (reflective, pacing) I know... you are right, but we never accepted that truth, at least I never did. Now I am beginning to wonder... how did he know so much... must be the guru he used to talk about. I wish I had one like that. (pause, then anxiety) But what a mystery with Raju... I can't figure out... All those letters, no reply. I feel as if he lead me on to the hill, from where I can see more... Then all of a sudden... Raju no more. What happened to that boy? Where has he disappeared? We have to find out, we must.

Gauri: Have faith, one day we will find him... for your sake.

John: (resigned) Well... soon, I hope. (recompose) And where are the kids? It's so quiet...

Gauri: Well, Misha was practicing piano a while ago; then they were both watching TV; they must have gone to sleep by now.

John: Do you think I am ignoring them?... (comes closer) Am I ignoring you?

(Misha and Vicki walk in- dressed in pajamas)

Gauri: Aren't you sleeping yet? It is getting late now.

Misha: Don't worry, Mom. It's not too late. We are watching good show on PBS, called "nature through animals' eyes". About how different animals see different colors; some see in the dark; some have binocular vision. They are so different from us... our eyes are so different.

Vicki: Didi, whose eyes are the best... that can see everything?

Misha: I don't know that. Maybe, nobody can.

John: And even if you can see everything... You believe what you see.

Gauri: I am sure, if Raju was here, he would have a right answer for that.

Vicki: I am angry with Raju for not writing to us... not replying to any of my letters.

Gauri: Don't be angry bete, maybe he is busy with his studies. (to John) Listen, I have an idea. Why don't we try to make a phone call to his school... we might find out something about him.

John: That's a good idea. (looks at his watch) It will be about 9 in the morning there. The school should be open. Let us call the principal. (to Misha) Bete, do you remember the name of his school?

Misha: I remember... He used to talk about Krishna High School in Mathura.

(Vicki goes near Gauri, shows his pinki, and exits stage.)

John: OK, give me the phone. (moves around with chordless phone. mumbles country code, etc) Hello, hello... Please give me directory assistance in Mathura... Hello, yes, Mathura? OK, please give me the number for Krishna High School.

(John waits, writes down the number- 81049. Dials again for the school. Gauri and Misha watching anxiously, and find things to do in duress during the subsequent phone conversation between John and Munshi. John makes several attempts; finally the phone rings. Spot appears on Munshi Principal's secretary with desk and phone on the opposite side of stage; rays of sun filtering through the window. Gauri and Misha do not hear Munshi dialogues. Munshi moves around the table when irritated. John trembles and moves with chordless phone when he is losing hope of finding Raju)

Munshi: (yawning; flipping the register; reluctantly gets ready to pick up the phone) Hellooo... who is Speaking?

John: (some relief) Good morning, sir. This is a foreign call. Are you speaking from Krishna High School in Mathura?

Munshi: (cheerful) Very good morrning. He..he..he, I am the very senior secretary of Mr. Principal. Who is calling, please, sir...

John: My name is Arjun Pandey.

Munshi: Who? Speak louder, please...

John: (trying to change his accent; louder) I am Arjun Pandey, calling from America.

Munshi: But your name is Indian only... why you are calling from Amreeka?

John: Because I live in America.

Munshi: May I ask why you are living in Amreeka? To where do you belong?

John: (irritated) Can I now tell you why I am calling.

Munshi: First, please tell me from where you are calling.

John: I am calling from America... I am a Senator here.

Munshi: What is the meaning of Seenaytor?

John: I mean... I am part of the American Congress.

Munshi: (stands up) Caangrace? Oh, I see... The Indian Caangrace party has opened office there too. Very ismart, very good. He..he..he.., changed name from Indian Caangrace to Amreekan Caangrace? And nobody here knows about it... hm

John: You are misunderstanding, sir.

Munshi: He..he..he.., (sitting down) that is quite alright. Everybody misunderstands the Caangrace, I am not alone. But, I am sure, they are quite popular in Amreeka. Isn't that so? And we all like Amreekan things too... Do you see Hindi filims? See the boys and girls jumping to Amreekan toon?

John: Sir, I have called to find about a boy in your school.

<u>Munshi:</u> I am really proud of you and your party... He..he..he.., which other party would care about a boy in our school?

<u>John:</u> Thank you, sir, thank you. Now, please tell me about Raju.

(Peon enters, places tea cup on table and departs. John becoming increasingly anxious)

<u>Munshi:</u> (taking a sip; gets annoyed) Pandeyji! Please wait a minute; I have a big energency here. (puts the phone down, yells at peon) Abay, Lakhanava! He..he.. he.., ye kya kiya toone re?

<u>Lakhan:</u> (returns scared) Kaa bhava maalik?

<u>Munshi:</u> (stands up) Array dekh, ye chai hai? Ya thandaee? Ekdam thandi... jaa garam kar ke laa. Jara jaldi ja, aur lapak ke aa.

<u>Lakhan:</u> (apologetic) Galti hoi gayee maalik. Bas dui minute...

<u>Munshi:</u> (points to phone) Maaloom hai, ye Amreeka se trunk call hai. (Lakhan looks impressed, departs with tea cup. Munshi sits down and resumes on phone) Haan Pandeyji... tau kya... Achha... Raju? Which Raju? There are many Rajus here. Don't you know that about 10 percent of Indian boys have Raju in their names. There are 7 Rajus in this ischool. About which Raju you are asking?

John: (impatiently) I am asking about my Raju.

Munshi: I am sure that you are very sure about your Raju. He..he..he.., but I am not so sure. tell me which Raju is your son?

John: Not my son, sir. He came to America during last summer.

Munshi: (irritated, gets up, talks fasy and loud) Really? But nobody told me about it. Which Raju went to Amreeka without telling me? What is his good name? To which place he belongs?

John: (mellows with concern) Sir, I must find out where Raju is. His full name is Rajesh Nandan Parthasarathy. He is 14 years old. He said he was born in Mathura. He lived with my family last summer, for two months- May and June. Your principal had sent him here.

Munshi: (stands up) Very interesting... principal saheb never told me anything about it (looks puzzled, then changes expression) He..he..he.., never mind, please tell me his name again... (cuts himself short as Lakhan returns with tea) Pandeyji! Just one minute, please wait, I have a very small emergency this time. (puts the phone down; slurps hot tea slowly but loudly; appears satisfied; picks up the phone; gestures Lakhan first OK for tea, them for him to depart; Lakhan departs. Munshi sits down) Yes Pandeyji! Let's taak. What was the boy's name again?

John: Rajesh Nandan Parthasarathy.

Munshi: Very long name, very beautiful name. He..he.. he.., please wait a moment. I will look (pause... tension builds. continues to search register, while sipping tea. calls Lakhan to remove tea cup. Finally, gestures failure to find the name) Bhai Pandeyji, he..he..he.., I am really very sorry. No boy in this school has such a beautiful, long name. I know nothing about your Raju.

John: Sir, you must. Please check again.

Munshi: (coldly) We don't have check, we only have register. And I have looked in the register... Wait, I will look in the last year's register also. (pause... more tension and disappointment) Pandeyji, again I am sorry... We never had any student in this school having that name. (warms up) Anyway, when you visit Mathura, I want to meet you; He..he..he.., and if you can remember, please bring one towel for me, the real thick one which is also the soft one... And listen, you may use your other sources to find that boy... Raju. I am sorry, I cannot help you. (puts the phone down) Haray Krishna... Haray Krishna... Arey Lakhanwa!

(Click sound, phone is disconnected, dial tone. Lights off Munshi; he exits. Flute music fades in, continues softly)

John: (looking at phone) That's impossible. I don't understand that... Where is Raju? Where is Raju? Where is Raju? (Misha takes the phone from John and puts it away)

Gauri: (hold his hands) Please calm down, let's think...

Misha: (suddenly looks amused, points to a spot in the audience) Look! Dad, what a surprise! Look there!

John: (feeling hopeless) Look at what?

Misha: Look at Raju, there... sitting in the audience... he didn't even tell us.

John: (looking in a different direction) Where's Raju?... Where?... Oh yes, now I can see... there. Come on Raju, why are you sitting there, smiling, and I went through such a pain trying to call your school in India.

(Gauri and Misha hold on to John, pointing in one direction, John still looking in another direction. Meanwhile Vicki returns and joins the confusion; he is holding flute in his left hand.)

Misha: Dad, Raju is there... not there!

John: (now looks in the same direction as pointed by Misha) You are right I see him there... But who is that (looking toward his previous gaze) That is also Raju. Which one is the real Raju? (more confused, pointing every which way. Gauri and Misha look puzzled. John becomes increasingly hysterical) Now... I see Raju everywhere. Everyone looks like Raju. No, it can't be. How can everybody out there have Raju's face? That makes no sense. I see hundreds of Rajus... but that's impossible. Where's Raju?... the real Raju... the one I need... Would someone please tell me? I need help... (Manthan music fades in; John feels relief) enjoy the music for 1 minute. That same music again! (music fades out; John still listening) for ½ minute. This silence is the music of peace... of happiness.

(Gauri and Misha come closer, keep holding John's hands for comfort. They are amazed at John's utterances. They appear sympathetic, though puzzled. Quiet.)

Vicki: (slowly walks up to John; silence evrywhere, speeks slowly but clearly) Daddy, I know a way... if you can not find Raju... the real Raju... then why don't you become your own Raju. That way, you will never lose him... never... right, dad?

(John nods... feels gentle relief... touches Vicki's head... still thoughtful. Gauri directs John's attention to rear stage. This is the finale of light and sound effects.

Spot on the back of Raju facing away at the hind door in rear stage. Manthan music fades in. Lights dim.

Raju slowly turns around facing the audience, while spot dims to off. Foot light in rear stage on Raju's back, only shows his profile in silhouette. Manthan music gets louder, then fades out after 10 seconds; only flute music is heard, now with rhythm and bells. Rays and flashes of light scattered around the auditorium. Flute music fades out after 10 seconds. Chorus humming fades in for 20 seconds, then fades out. Fusion music begins when curtain begins to close.

THE END